So Long As Love Remembers

Mary W. Cordel

DEDICATION

This book, SO LONG AS LOVE REMEMBERS, is dedicated to the memory of my beloved husband, Wilburn E. Cordell (1923-2004) and our beloved son, Dr. Gerald Dykes Cordell (1944-1996). Both will live in my heart so long as I remember.

Yesterday is a Memory
Tomorrow is a Hope
Today is the tie that
    binds them
Live all of your Todays
With a hope of Tomorrow
So that all of your Yesterdays
    Will be Happy
      Memories

Mary W. Cordell

CONTENTS

ACKNOWLEDGMENTS

I want to thank Alissa Beeler, a special niece, who took the time and trouble to produce a typed copy of the original journal I wrote in longhand, using the seven hundred love letters that were written between my husband and me during the four years we endured World War II.

I want to thank Christina Manning without whose help and expertise I could never have gotten my book ready for publishing and presentation to the public.

A special thanks to Glenda Owen, a dear friend who suggested the title for my book.

And to all the loving family and friends who encouraged me along the way and to all of those who will take the time to read my love story.

1 PROLOGUE: A SEPTEMBER NIGHT 2008

"Twilight is the loneliest time of the day", she thought, as she settled into the rocking chair on the back porch. It had not always been.

Her mind skittered back to the days when she would look forward to this time of the day. Days when she would stand at the window or the door, straining to hear the car coming up the driveway or hear the door slam as he got out and headed for the house. She would ease back into the dimness of the hallway so he wouldn't tease her about being so excited over his arrival. She knew it pleased him that they had never really lost that delicious thrill of seeing each other again - each time a new and special renewal of love and commitment.

Just to watch him coming up the walk, taking the porch steps two at a time as if he knew she was waiting for the right moment to rush herself out of the shadows and throw her arms around his neck, as if he had been away on a long journey. It did not matter that it had only been a few hours since she had hugged and kissed him goodbye that morning. The joy of being back together after the short separation had never palled through the years. Closing the door behind them, throwing his arm around her small shoulders, he felt again the wonder of her unfailing love. And she felt the absolute security and permanence of his.

Now she rocked alone, escaping the loneliness of the

too large home she inhabited by herself. Listening to the world as it drifted into the quiet of the dusk on the September night of 2008, she sighed.

The dusk to dawn light came on and with it the arrival of the small winged night moths that circled around it, the only visible form of life besides herself and she felt comforted by their presence. The town was quiet, an occasional automobile coming up the hill and quickly fading into the night. The sound of crickets filled the air and the lonesome hoot of the old owl who lived at the back of the yard let her know there were other living things around and that comforted her also. So she rocked alone, back and forth.

The rhythmic squish-squish of the rocker going back and forth on the boards of the porch reminded her of another similar rhythmic back and forth movement on another September night in 1941. She was seated on a front porch in a white wicker chair, settled on the upholstered seat, feeling the roughness of the cretonne cushion rubbing against the back of her knees. And in front of her, the matching wicker swing with a matching cretonne cushion was making a squish-squish sound as two pair of long male legs pushed it gently back and forth.

She sat there on that front porch on Sweetbriar Street in Nashville, thinking of the bookkeeping lesson she had to complete before she could go to bed. And she was wondering, "Why are they here? What do they want from me?" She had only met them once before in April of that year when the younger one, Wilburn Cordell, had come to Pulaski to see a girl he knew there and had persuaded Donald Robinson, who was a year older and had a car, to drive him down. The girl, Joyce, had persuaded her to go on a blind date with Donald. But the morning after that meeting, she was back in her little world of getting ready for high school graduation and writing her Valedictorian speech. So she had almost forgotten about the two boys and the three hours they drove around the surrounding highways and byways. But then when she came to Nashville in the Fall, having received a scholarship from Nashville Business College, Wilburn had kept insisting that Joyce write to her and ask her to call. So she finally did and now they were sitting there taking up her time when she should be studying.

The two very handsome males, who occupied the swing seemed to also be uncertain as to just why they were there. The younger one, Wilburn, was six months shy of his nineteenth birthday and he seemed to be the one interested in being there. She could not help but stare at him as the street light from Hillsboro Road cast a sort of glow around him and by the side of him the older boy was more in the shadow. She knew from the other time she had seen them that while Donald was good looking, his looks paled when he sat next to Wilburn.

She couldn't decide if they were still boys or were they men? She was eighteen and she still felt young and naïve and she couldn't decide just where to place them.

She leaned forward and said, "Do you have to work tonight, Wilburn?" sort of hoping that he did so they would soon be gone. She knew that he worked nights for the railroad at Union Station as Joyce had told her.

"No", he said, "I am off tonight but I don't go to work until 11 PM when I am working. I get off at 7 AM and sleep most of the day. " She knew that from the conversation she had had with his Mother when she finally called to see why he was asking Joyce to tell her to call. He had given his mother orders to wake him up if she called and the first time she talked with him he sort of bawled her out for waiting so long to get in touch.

She noticed how his black hair was brushed back off of a strong broad forehead and the waves were formed as if they were glued in place. An errant curl escaped to fall across his forehead. He kept pushing it back but it had a mind of its own. Black eyebrows formed perfect arches over dark brown eyes, the eyebrows almost coming together over a straight patrician nose. The jaw was squared and a beautifully formed mouth made a slash above it. He smiled as she stared and his teeth were straight and white as pearls. Her own eyes seemed to be mesmerized on his handsome face and she forced them to travel on down to the broad shoulders, the muscled forearms bulging beneath the pristine white shirt. She thought, "Goodness, he looks like a Greek God."

Years later she thought she must have fallen in love at that very moment but she was too sheltered and too innocent to understand the feeling.

The swing went back and forth as did the mundane conversation. They really did not know each other well enough to talk about anything meaningful. But it was not her nature to be quiet for very long so every time the dialogue floundered, she jumped in with some kind of silly chatter.

All of a sudden, Donald announced they needed to go. Wilburn left the swing as Donald did and she arose and walked to the top step, still wondering why these two handsome specimens had called to see if they could come over. And why had she said, "OK"?

When they reached the bottom step, and she had almost gone through the front door, hurrying to get to the waiting homework, Wilburn turned and asked, "Would you go to a party with me this Friday night?" She answered, "I would like that."

So that was how it began on a lovely September night in 1941.

Pulling her thoughts back to the present, she rocked a little longer , brushed her graying hair back from her face and placed her aging hands on the arms of the rocker for leverage, so she could stand. Suddenly she saw wings flapping lazily, coming toward the light. She caught her breath as she had never seen a more beautiful moth. She sat very still so as not to frighten it away and she watched as the moth settled itself on the back of her left hand that rested on the chair arm. It had a wing span of almost two inches, yellow and black coloring on the wings. They shone with the beam of the porch light outlining the inner parts of the bright yellow wings with the black threads running through them as if someone had taken a black marker and drawn wavy lines through the yellow. The edges of the wings had been touched with light brown all around. It took her breath away.

It sat there, stroking its eyes with its spidery front legs, seeming to deliberate what to do next. Then slowly the wings moved and it flew up to her face and settled itself on her mouth. She sat so still, fascinated by the soft creature who had come to visit. She felt its wing move very softly across her lips, a touch like a feather, as it sipped at the moisture formed at the edge of her mouth. Unhurried, it sat and sipped. Then she felt again the velvety wing softly caress her kips and then a third time, slowly, gently with no pressure against her mouth. Finally it rose into the air and flew gracefully into the darkness.

She reached up and touched her lips, tentatively, impressed by the gentleness of the kiss of the moth's wings. She had touched her lips the same way that Friday night in September, 1941 when Wilburn had touched her lips with his, no pressure, no demands, a kiss as light as a feather or the brush of a moth's wings, not once but three times, as if he were sipping nectar from a rare and exotic flower, as the moth had done this night.

She sat a little longer and let her mind dwell on the sweetness of that first date, but she knew she did not dare let herself go too far back into that long ago time of love, war, sadness and joy or she would not be able to sleep at all.

She reminded herself, as she had so many times - nothing of the past is truly lost even if it can only be recaptured in thought, even if it comes only in snatches of memory that flickers like shadows across a screen or is triggered by a sound that brings back something that happened so long ago, a word said, a whispered avowal of love, a treasured longing. No, nothing is truly gone or lost...................

So Long As Love Remembers...

2 APRIL 1941

1941........Having just clawed their way out of the hole of
the Depression years, Americans were beginning to see
their way to better living and prosperity. There were wars
and rumors of wars in Europe but Americans were not
interested in getting involved. Had they not fought the War
to end all wars and closed the door to any more
involvements in 1918? We were all dedicated to
Isolationism. It did not matter that Hitler was spreading his
spider web of hatred and oppression on the smaller
countries in Europe. What did we care if Japan had taken
over a large portion of China? America was on a roll and
thumbing our noses at the rest of the world. We had been
through ten years of deprivation and now that we were back
on our feet no one could stop our progress!

After the failure of the Stock Market in October, 1929
things had gone from bad to worse and by October 24th of
that year the panic was on, stocks were worthless, banks
closed down, people lost all of their money they had in
banks.

Some bank presidents shot themselves, some people
jumped out of tall building windows. And of course,
President Herbert Hoover was blamed for it all. When
President Hoover was inaugurated in March, 1929, the
future had appeared bright for a prosperous America. By
December of that year, American businessmen and farmers

were facing the most difficult business crisis in the U. S. history.

In 1930 U. S. population was 123,203,000. Sinclair Lewis was the first American to win the Nobel Prize in Literature for his novel BABBITT. Also a book called THE STRANGE DEATH OF PRESIDENT HARDING was a best seller. It presented the theory that Harding had been poisoned by his wife.

In 1931, Herbert Hoover signed an act making "The Star Spangled Banner" our National Anthem. In March of 1931, in Scottsboro, Alabama, nine black youths were charged and convicted of rape. They were known as "The Scottsboro Boys". They were later vindicated and released after years of confinement. That case paved the way for black people to serve on juries.

In 1932, unemployment had reached 13 million and wages were 60% less than they were in 1929. "Brother, Can You Spare A Dime?" was a popular song. Charles Lindbergh, Jr. was kidnapped on March 3, 1932 and his body was found two months later on the Lindbergh Estate. Five thousand Federal agents had been under direct order of the President to search for the little boy. America grieved with the Lindbergh's. A typical reaction to the little boy's murder was that." Christ died for the sins of the World. Was it possible little Charles died for the sins of America?"

We had marches then with thousands of people marching against Prohibition. Labor Unions demonstrated wanting jobs. In July, 1932, Franklin Delano Roosevelt , Democratic candidate for President , pledged a "New Deal" for Americans. In July of that year, after camping in paper shacks for a month near the U. S. Capitol, thousands of veterans demanding a bonus were attacked by police and U. S. Army units commanded by General Douglas MacArthur. Two members of the Brown Army were killed.

On September 12, 1932 a large crowd of unemployed in Toledo, Ohio marched on grocery stores and seized food. They were near starvation after County authorities cut off relief.

On November 8, 1932 Franklin D. Roosevelt was

elected President. When he took office there were reportedly 67,000 homeless children roaming the streets of New York City. In Roosevelt's first 100 days numerous Federal Agencies were created to deal with the pervasive crisis. He began to wage war against the inequities and resentments that bred the feelings of revolution in America.

On the other side of the world, another face appeared on the scene. On January 30, 1932 President van Hindenburg of Germany appointed Adolf Hitler Chancellor . On Hitler's 44th birthday, April 20, millions of Germans paraded to the Nazi song," When Blood Flows From Our Knives".

In December, 1933 Prohibition was repealed.

1934 was a year of Union strikes in every large company hiring thousands of people. There were Teamster strikes, Longshoremen strikes, Electrician strikes, Railroad strikes, Mine strikes and so on. The National Guard and police forces assaulted the strikers to subdue the fighting between the strikers and the "scabs" who were crossing the picket lines so they could work.

Nevada, Utah and California were shaken by earthquakes. The only fatality was a woman who died of fright.

One day a 66 year old physician in California, watched as three elderly women scrounged through garbage for food. That physician formed the Townsend Club and put out a publication called The Townsend National Weekly. In no time thousands of people signed up for membership and the publication very quickly had a circulation of 200,000 papers weekly. This movement spurred Congress to enact Social Security in 1935.

These were the days I remember. I remember the Depression, the hard times people had. I remember the adults talking about losing all of their savings, having to go back home after moving away to a better life. I remember my parents leaving a defunct U-Haul It and Car Rental business he had in Decatur, Alabama and we moved to Cleveland, Ohio to try to find a job. I remember the day he came home with the news that the company he had worked for for two years had closed and his job was gone again. I remember moving back to the South, where there was family who would take us in until Daddy could get settled again.

I remember the years in Prospect, Tennessee where we rented a big two story house from an elderly lady who had been forced to go live with her children. I remember the first Christmas in Prospect when my brother, Jimmy, and I got a stocking each with one orange, a few nuts and a stalk of dried raisins. He got a cap pistol and some caps and I got a balsam wood airplane, about 3 inches long, with a heavy nose. We spent the day with me throwing my airplane in the air, Jimmy aiming at it and shooting a cap and the plane shooting another cap when it landed nose first. That Christmas stands out as one of the happiest I remember. That was the Christmas of 1932.

In 1935 Joe Louis knocked out heavyweight champion, Max Baer. I remember us listening to that fight over a little battery powered radio. That victory brought so much pride to black people that black athletes began to be noticed as worthy competitors.

In 1936, James Owens, a black man, won four gold medals at the Olympics in Berlin. This was a disappointment to Adolph Hitler as he had planned for these games to be a showcase that would prove the Aryan race and Nazi system was superior to all others.

Hitler was already planning and instituting his eventual takeover of the World. Fascist forces led by General Francisco Franco started the Spanish Civil War and was aided by German bombers and Italian troops.

But America was becoming more solvent and Franklin D. Roosevelt was elected for a second term in 1936. It was estimated that a half million people took part in sit-down strikes in America from September 1936 to May, 1937. But they were finally successful in organizing labor unions in General Motors and Chrysler Detroit factories. The masses prevailed against police forces and National Guard troops. This was really democracy in action. The people joined together to accomplish what they wanted.

The new year of the new decade found our family in good shape financially. My father, Cecil Whitlock, had managed to get the capital to purchase his own Filling Station, my brother was finishing up two years of college and would soon be home to help with the business. I was finishing up high school that Spring and was on the way to be valedictorian of the class and hoping for a scholarship to a school away from home. I loved my family and my three little sisters, but felt I needed to get away.

None of us had any inkling of what the year would bring as we tripped happily along with our brand new lives. Franklin Delano Roosevelt had been elected to an unprecedented third term as President and we all felt that he would safely lead us for the next four years.

So April, 1941 came and I reached the ripe old age of eighteen on the twenty fourth day of that month. And how could I imagine that I was soon to meet my future?

3 FIRST MEETING

How do you define a day in which your whole life changes?

Maybe you were not aware of it at the time but as things develop you look back and can pinpoint almost the exact time that something so unexpected happened and your life took a new direction. For me a Friday, April 26, 1941, was just such a day.

I was two days past my eighteenth birthday and I was giddy with the excitement of Life. It was a school day as usual and only one more month until I would be on my way to adulthood. I was always old for my age anyway but I just knew something great was awaiting me somewhere out there.

So that afternoon I was sitting in the "parlor" just thinking and planning. Mama was in the kitchen getting things ready for our main meal of the day – supper. The three little sisters were outside playing and traffic was steady on Highway 64 but I was smug and comfortable sitting on the sofa and dreaming, one eye on the girls playing in the front yard but my mind on far away expectations.

I saw her coming up the street, a girl I went to school and also church with. She was just sixteen and not someone I hung out with. In fact, I did not do much hanging out. I was too studious and busy helping Mama with the girls to have much time for running around with the other girls.

To me, they seemed rather silly, giggling and whispering about the boys all the time.

I wondered what Joyce was coming for but got up to meet her as she came up the porch steps. I knew her well enough to know that she had been dating a boy from Nashville and that he was a couple of years older than she was. I knew her father had died when she was little and she was raised by her mother and grand-mother. But that was all I knew. She was not what you would call really pretty but she looked okay. None of us had money at that time to spend on a lot of beauty products and fancy clothes. She always looked clean and neat. She was going to be stocky built as she got older but for sixteen she certainly looked all right.

"Hi!", I said, holding the screen door open. "Come on in. I have to sit where I can see the little girls playing so we will just sit here on the couch." Mama hollered from the kitchen to say, "Hi" to Joyce. We were close enough we could hear her rattling pots and pans as she worked and she could hear us talking. After a few words of conversation about the weather and other mundane things, Joyce got to the point of her visit.

"Wilburn is coming down from Nashville tonight and bringing another boy with him. I need someone to go along with us and I thought about you. Will you go?

"Well,, I don't know," I replied. I did not want her to think I was snooty but I really didn't care about blind dates. So I told her just that. "I'm not much for blind dates." I was always afraid the blind date would be disappointed with me.

Now Mama never encouraged me to date or to try to attract boys. She would have been happy to have all five of her children remain single and at home forever. So I was really surprised when she walked out of the kitchen, wiping her hands on her apron, and said, "I do not know why you won't go. You never go anywhere."

That was so unusual and unlike my mother that I said before I thought, "Well, OK, I will go". That made Joyce happy and she left telling me they would pick me up around 7 PM.

I had a new dress, olive and white striped, with a bright yellow jacket. I also had new spectator pumps with high heels. Now those spectator pumps could make me feel like a million dollars. They were white with brown trim around the soles and the high heels in brown leather and with nail head sized indentations decorating the toes and around the instep. I had worked for three Saturdays at the dry cleaners to be able to afford them and I really felt dressed up that night. Besides the heels added two or three inches to my height and I needed that as I was only about five feet two inches tall and weighed about 105 pounds. My long hair cooperated for a change and with my new clothes I really felt good about myself as I waited to be picked up. They arrived shortly after 7 PM.

The boy who came with Wilburn was named Donald. He was nineteen and he owned the car. So he and I sat in the front seat. He was very nice looking and I was glad Mama had persuaded me to go with them. I would turn sideways every once in a while and talk to Wilburn and Joyce. We all sat far apart - there was no snuggling or petting going on. Just four young people having a good time. I wondered how Joyce had attracted a boy as handsome as Wilburn. He was six foot tall, broad shouldered, black wavy hair and brown eyes that seemed to look into your soul. He had a broad forehead, straight patrician nose and a square rather stubborn looking chin. Donald was a good looking boy but he faded into the background beside Wilburn.

We drove down into Alabama, stopped someplace and had a coke then drove back up a country road to a small settlement, called Pettusville, Alabama. I had friends there and my parents had lived there when I was three years old. So we stopped for a while to visit with my friend, Bob Dunnavant. I had known him all my life as we had mutual cousins. He was a fun kind of guy and he played a guitar. We all sat on the front porch and sang and joked and laughed a lot. I had to be home by 10 PM so we headed on back to Pulaski.

When we got to the Square we still had about fifteen

minutes before my curfew. So we parked at the Courthouse and the boys got out to toss a coin. This was to decide if they would go back home or drive down to Fort Benning, Georgia to check on a boy from Nashville who had enlisted in the Army and was stationed there. The Georgia trip won out and I was rather disgusted that something of that magnitude could be decided with a toss of a coin. I felt that Georgia was in another country.

If anyone had told me when Donald escorted me up the steps to our porch that night and I waved goodbye to Wilburn and Joyce waiting in the car and thanked Donald for the nice ride, that I had met the man I was going to spend my life with, I would have laughed them to scorn as I was simply not impressed.

Oh, what a fragile thread our Destiny hangs on!

4 SPRING & SUMMER OF 1941

Looking back, I wonder why I did not awaken to great fanfare after my first encounter with the man of my dreams. There should have been bells ringing, a band playing, balloons filling the sky and I would have been walking on air. Instead it was a very ordinary morning in our happy and noisy household.

Mama was always up at the crack of dawn and we all awoke to smells of breakfast being prepared in the kitchen. We were very orderly in our sharing of the bathroom. Of course, Daddy had first access and then my brother, Jimmy, would have been next. But this Saturday, he had stayed in Nashville where he had one more month before graduating from David Lipscomb College. I always shared the bathroom with the three little sisters, Paula, Peggy and Nancye, ages 11, 8 and 4. I did various things for them. helping them to get dressed for the day, performing my own requirements for being presentable for the day.

We all assembled to eat together and everyone talked at once. It was always a lot of fun to share a meal as a family. Daddy left to open his Service Station, a block from where we lived. I left shortly after to walk to my Saturday job at Sunshine Cleaners. I had been trained to alter men's pants so that was my main job. But I could also meet the public and accept the clothes they brought to be cleaned. Mrs. Ara Springer owned the Cleaners and she was very sweet to me.

I think I earned about $I.50 a day, but I had an NRA job at school working in the school office and that paid $3.50 a month. The NRA was part of Franklin D. Roosevelt's program to bring us out of the Depression. I bought lots of things for my sisters and myself and I could pay for them at fifty cents a week. I was always very careful to keep my good credit rating.

I was very busy the last week of April and the first three weeks of May, 1941 because I had to write and practice my Valedictory Speech. I was also Editor-in-Chief of our School Annual and that had taken up a lot of my time and was ready for sale and disposition at school.

I was making plans to work all summer and then go to Nashville in September to take advantage of the scholarship I had been offered at Nashville Business College. I had always intended to be a teacher but Daddy had just purchased the Service Station, my brother was just finishing his two years of College, so Daddy could not afford for me to go away to college. They wanted me to stay at home and go to Martin College but I wanted to get out into the world so I finally persuaded them to let me go. They really had no choice as my destiny was in Nashville and things were moving in the direction of the plot for my life.

I was a little worried about it as I had always thought I would be a teacher and I had not taken any business courses in High School. No typing, no shorthand, no bookkeeping. I was proficient in English, Civics, History, Math and Languages. I was also worried because I would have to live with a strange family and work for my board. The College would place me so I did not have a choice as to who I would live with. But my course was set and I hid my concerns and started working toward moving to Nashville that Fall.

1941 was filled with apprehension because of Hitler's War in Europe. Roosevelt was elected for an unprecedented third term. He wanted America to become what he termed as "the great arsenal of democracy" in the fight against Hitlerism. Americans wanted to stay isolated from the War but our friend, Great Britain, was pushing us to help them. Roosevelt felt that we must be involved but for a while he did no more than institute the Lend Lease which enabled us to help Britain with military supplies and ammunition. We also gave aid three months later to Russia when they were attacked by the Germans. But we still felt that we were safe from having to send our young men to fight. But the net was closing that would bring us closer to having to do so.

Because of that, there were a lot of troop movements during the Spring and Summer of 1941. We lived on the corner of Fifth Street and Highway 64, which was the main highway between Chattanooga and Memphis. There would be convoys coming through Pulaski for periods of ten to twelve hours at a time – trucks loaded with soldiers, supplies, equipment, jeeps and other war materials. These soldiers would toss out their addresses at those of us who stood in our yards and porches to wave at them and cheer, and also gather up the addresses so we could write to them and keep up morale. On one week end in May I was on the front porch doing just that and I picked out one address to correspond with. His name was W. H. Davis and he was 28 years old. He sent me a big Teddy Bear from Seattle and a nice compact with a map of Alaska drawn on the front from Alaska where he was finally stationed. We corresponded all summer but it meant nothing to me other than the fact that I was doing my part for the "boys". W. H. was from Smyrna, Tennessee.

Jimmy's graduation was May 25th and our whole family made the trip to Nashville for the day. For about the entire two years Jimmy was at Lipscomb, I had more or less been his roommate's girl. When there was a play or ballgame at Lipscomb, Benny would invite me to come up. I would always stay in the girl's dorm with his first cousin, Frances. It was fun to do every once in a while. I would have to ride the train or bus up there and back. So I was with Benny and the family that day. Benny also graduated. Wilburn was also at Lipscomb that day as his brother, John Alton, was graduating too. If I saw Wilburn I did not recognize him. He told me later that he saw me but did not speak as I seemed to be pretty involved. Why on Earth did the Sun not stop in its tracks, or bugles blow and a band come marching by when I was that close to my future and was so unaware of his presence?

Summer passed slowly as usual when you are stretching toward the future as I was at eighteen. I worked all Summer, bought clothes for school and squirreled back as much change as I could to have for spending money in Nashville. I had learned the importance of a dime a few years back when I was fourteen and we were deep into the Big Depression. One morning before Daddy left for work, I asked for a dime for notebook paper as I was down to my last sheet. To this day, I see his face when he had to tell me, "Hon, I don't have a dime to my name." It broke my heart to see the regret and sadness in his blue eyes. And I vowed to never be wasteful with paper again as long as I lived. I borrowed paper from a friend to make it through the week and repaid her when I got a pack after Daddy got paid on Saturday night. I have always paid back anything I owed first and if anything is left I feel free to spend it.

But Summer ended and I was in Nashville. I was assigned to work for a family named Martin. Mr. Martin traveled all week but was home on weekends. My job was basically to be a Nanny to their three little boys, all preschoolers and a maid, cook and housekeeper to a rather fragile Mrs. Martin. I had Saturday afternoons and all day Sunday free and they were happy for me to go home at those times whenever I could as that gave them time forj just family. My small bedroom was upstairs with the boys room close by. My job after school until 8 PM was to look after the boys, get them fed and bathed and into bed. After that, I could study, read or whatever. Then I helped Mrs. Martin get them dressed and fed before I left for school each morning. There was not much time for just socializing.

Then Wilburn was back in the picture and my destiny began to unfold. And it all came to pass because he maneuvered it to happen and I really had no say in the matter. It was just meant to be as so many things are in Life. We only realize the fact when we look back and remember.

5 BEGINNING BUSINESS COLLEGE

The first two or three weeks in Nashville were a mixed bag of excitements, frustrations, getting used to more people and traffic, making new friends at the Business College, getting used to three little boys instead of three sisters and a certain amount of homesickness. But I soon settled in and developed a system that made it possible for me to do the menial duties required for earning my room and board and making friends with the Martin boys, Junior, Jackie, and Johnny.

It was obvious that Mrs. Martin was from money and the proverbial "raised with a silver spoon" would have applied to her. But she was nice enough, careful not to get too chummy but easy to get along with as long as the work was done to her standards. That was not hard for me as my Mother was a meticulous housekeeper and I had never been allowed to slack on my household duties. That was where the resemblance ended as my Mother never expected anyone to do more than she was willing to do and having been raised as the tenth of twelve children, she was not used to anything that even looked like a "silver spoon".

With Mr. Martin away during the week days, there was not a lot of cooking to do. Mrs. Martin liked to prepare the weekend meals herself while Mr. Martin was at home. I especially remember her preparing a delicious stuffed fish. Later in life I wished I had paid more attention to how she did that.

I did not get to go home for about a month. But I received three letters the first two weeks from Joyce asking me to call Wilburn and let him know where I was living as Donald wanted to come to see me. At first I paid no attention to her request as girls did not call boys, especially when they had only met the one time. But after the third request I decided it would not hurt me to call and see what was going on. So about the third Saturday I was in Nashville, I made the call that would change my life – in fact my very reason for being.

My Mother would have disapproved of my calling any boy I did not know personally but Joyce was getting a little huffy at me as Wilburn kept asking her to get me to call. I always had free time from the Martin chores from noon Saturday until Monday morning. When Mr. Martin was home, he did a lot of the tending to the boys as well as helping his wife cook.

The call was answered by a very sweet sounding woman, Mother Cordell. When I asked for Wilburn she told me he was sleeping as he worked nights at the railroad.

"Oh, I'm sorry, don't wake him up", I told her wishing I had not called. Then she asked who was calling and when I told her, she said, "I'm supposed to wake him if you call". I was more puzzled than ever as to why my calling was so important.

I waited while she roused him from sleep and the first time I ever really talked to him, he bawled me out for not calling sooner. I hung up thinking, "Who does he think he is?" but I had agreed that he and Donald could come over the following Tuesday night after I got the boys to bed.

They came. We sat on the front porch with the two of them on the swing and me sitting across from them in the wicker rocker. The conversation was stilted at first and then we all three seemed to relax and we discussed movies we had seen, how I liked the Business College and what did I think of Nashville and how did I like being part of a strange family? I realized later that most of the conversation was aimed at finding out all about me and what I liked. I was sort of confused as it was apparent Donald was not interested in me. It seemed he had just brought Wilburn over.

When they got ready to leave, Wilburn asked me if I would go to a party with him Friday night. I thought for a few minutes and finally said, "Yes, I would like that." He smiled and said he would pick me up at 8 PM. I knew he would have to be at work by 11 PM so I was sure I would be home by 10 PM.

It was hard for me to get my mind focused on the bookkeeping problem I had to solve before I could go to bed. I kept seeing in my mind that handsome Wilburn Cordell. I thought he was the most handsome boy I had ever met and certainly the best looking one who had ever asked me for a date. He was kind of movie star handsome and I was not a little perplexed over his asking me out.

But the bells were still not ringing nor were the stars exploding or balloons in the air for me..

6 FIRST KISS

Friday night came and I was ready to be picked up by 8 PM. I felt confused and a little aggravated at myself for saying "Yes" to the invitation. I really did not feel that I was encroaching on Joyce's territory. It was only a party and we would be with a crowd of teenagers. But it was foreign to my nature to go out with someone I hardly knew. Then I would decide, "Oh, well after tonight I will probably never hear from him again".

Just before I was about to call and back out about going, he arrived. This time, Thomas Hamlett brought him as Wilburn still did not have a car of his own. Thomas was a year older than Wilburn and me. Most of Wilburn's good friends were older. Thomas was one of his best friends and the three of us became a threesome most of the time until Thomas found a girl he wanted. But that came later.

The party was in full swing when we got there. And by full swing, I mean they were really swinging. It was a two story apartment and no parents were there. It seemed that one or two of the girls lived there on their own. I never asked. I knew the moment we went in that I was in the wrong place at the wrong time. We were late getting there and several of the boys had been hitting the bottle pretty steadily. One or two had passed out and the other boys had them upstairs trying to sober them up with cold water. The radio was blaring and the couples were dancing and laughing and having a ball

I found a chair in the corner and tried to disappear. I wondered what I could do. I had no money for cab fare. And Wilburn was the only one I knew by name except Thomas and I barely knew them. I have to admit that neither of them took the drinks they were offered and I certainly didn't. But I was sitting in the corner, bombarded by the loud music and boisterous laughter and the boy upstairs cussing the others who were trying to sober him up. I just knew someone was going to call the law and what would I tell my mother? I would be moved back home immediately whether I wanted to be or not.

After fifteen minutes of almost abject terror, I told Wilburn he would have to take me home. I knew I was ruining his night but what else could I do? He did not question my decision. He borrowed Thomas's car and we headed for Sweetbriar Street and safety.

I hated to be a wet blanket so I chattered about some kind of nonsense all the way home, trying to justify the fact that I could not stay at that kind of party. Finally, it dawned on me that he didn't really care whether we stayed or not. He had certainly not participated in the rabble rousing. So he just let me ramble on until we arrived at my destination. Then I started trying to apologize for ruining his night. And right in the middle of a sentence, he leaned over and kissed me on the lips, a kiss as light as a feather. I sat there dumbfounded. I had been kissed a few times before but had always seen it coming and managed to turn my cheek. My mother had told me that nice girls did not let boys kiss them. I got real still and quiet. I did not know what to say. Then he leaned over again and put his lips to mine. It was not a demanding kiss, no pressure at all. I still did not move or say anything. But when the third kiss, soft and still undemanding, touched my lips and left me wanting more, I managed to get out of the car. He was by my side immediately and walked me to the door. I think we both said, "Goodnight" but I could never be sure.

I had trouble going to sleep as I could not figure out just what had happened. It seemed I could hear bells ringing at a far distance and when I closed my eyes I could see distant stars twinkling but there was no band, no balloons in the air. Anyway I probably would never see him again after making such a mess of things. He wrote me in a letter as time progressed that he knew that night that he had a girl his mother and older sister would approve of.

Had I turned out to be the kind of girl who would have stayed at the party and enjoyed being there, it would very likely have been our only date. But after that, he was always there. He lost no time in buying his own car. Sometimes he would show up after working all night to take me downtown to school. Sometimes being there in the afternoon to take me home. I could not understand but I was nice to him. And he treated me like a porcelain doll. Then I got skittish. He was much more than I wanted. And I felt pushed and upset over it. I would have something else planned if he asked me out. And sometimes I would go. Sometimes I avoided his calls but he still showed up. As I learned through the years, when Wilburn Cordell wanted something really bad he did not stop until he got it. And for some strange reason he wanted me.

I still thank the Lord that he was persistent or else I would have missed out on the best thing that ever happened to me.

7 FALL & WINTER 1941

The Fall of 1941 was a busy exciting time for me. I had really fallen in love with the studies required by the Business College. I quickly conquered typing and shorthand and was beginning to understand money management better with the bookkeeping homework.

I was excited because I was so busy all the time. In addition to school and the chores I had to accomplish at the Martin household, I had a busy social life.

Wilburn and Thomas were around any time I could be free to go somewhere. They would take me to Pulaski on the weekends Wilburn was not working. At that time, he would go see Joyce and Thomas and I would visit with my folks.

I had kept up the correspondence with W. H. Davis. One day, out of the blue, I got a call from his brother, Tommy, and he asked me if I would like to go to a movie. I accepted and was pleasantly surprised when he showed up. He was 18, the same age Wilburn and I were, and he was very good looking. It seemed that W. H. had asked him to look after me in Nashville. So we became friends and one week end he took me to Smyrna to meet the Davis family. They were having a family reunion and W. H. wanted me to meet all of them. They all lived in the vicinity where Mother and Dad Cordell had grown up. So the families knew each other.

I knew Wilburn did not want me to go out with Tommy

but I refused to be told what I could do. So he had to accept that but he tried to be available every chance he got.

The nation was on tenterhooks by October of 1941. The Newsreels at the movies brought us pictures of Hitler's atrocities against the Jews. Germany was engulfing all of the smaller countries in Europe. Russia started out being friendly with Germany and turning a blind eye to what was happening. But when Germany aimed their guns at Russia, they geared up to fight.

Great Britain was being badly hammered by Germany and on August 3rd President Roosevelt had announced he was going on a "fishing trip" off Martha's Vineyard, Mass. But it was really a meeting with Winston Churchill at Placentia Bay, Newfoundland. There they signed the Atlantic Compact. That defined the common war aims of the two countries.

Japan had invaded and taken over a part of China but Roosevelt was sure he could pacify Japan and persuade them to draw back from trying to take over more of that part of the world. Japan was spreading southward in the Pacific to establish the "Greater East Asia Co-Prosperity Sphere". Roosevelt assured Churchill that he could "baby Japan along for 3 more months." He hoped to do so by negotiating with them.

By October everyone was getting nervous over the possibility of being drawn into the War and we were all looking to Roosevelt to keep us out of it. Some of Wilburn's 19 year old friends were enlisting in the Army and he and I went to a Farewell Party for one of them one night in mid October. It was at a park area in East Nashville and as usual, he and I left before the party really got started. He had his own car by then so we were alone.

It is strange how vividly you remember your surroundings and your feelings about happenings from so long ago. But I see us as if it were yesterday, driving down Broadway in Nashville with me sitting well on my side of the car. We were passing in front of Union Station when Wilburn looked over at me and asked, "What would you say if I asked you to marry me?"

Well, that was a shock as I was still in the process of getting to know him. It was less than a month since I had gone to the first party with him. I hardly knew what to say. So I foolishly answered, "I guess I would laugh". How could I know he was serious? It was a while before he mentioned that again.

The phrase "Our hearts were light and gay" would have been appropriate for those halcyon days of October and November. Life went on as usual for most Americans, blissfully unaware that all through November Japan was carefully plotting an event that would change all of our lives overnight. I often wonder if we would have behaved differently had we known what was coming.

I was able to go home for the Thanksgiving weekend. Jimmy as at home, working at the station with Daddy, trying to save money enough for further education. I was glad to have the time at home with all of us there. I think Wilburn came down that Sunday afternoon to take me back to Nashville. So we sailed into the first week of December totally unaware of the tsunami that was soon to hit.

I felt more comfortable with Wilburn the more I was around him. He was jealous of Tommy Davis but I just let it slide over me and he stopped saying anything about it. I only saw Tommy about twice a month and I realized he was just a watchdog that his big brother had enlisted. But I did not share that with Wilburn. It was kind of nice for a handsome boy to be jealous over me.

On Sunday, December 7, 1941, the sun rose in the east just as it had for centuries. The Martin household was busy getting ready for church just like every other ordinary Sunday. I could walk to Hillsboro Church of Christ which I did. The Martins went to the church of their choice but we all came back to Sweetbriar Street for lunch. I helped to clear the table and clean up the kitchen. Mr. Martin turned the radio on in the living room. It was almost 1 PM Washington time. The announcer was screaming that our fleet at Pearl Harbor, Hawaii was being attacked by Japanese planes. We gathered around the radio and stayed glued to it most of the afternoon. That terrible news was all that was being broadcast. We learned later that 368 Japanese planes came out of nowhere at 7:33 AM Honolulu time and our base was caught totally unawares. The base was just waking up. Most of the pilots were on leave. Their planes had been lined up side by side to prevent sabotage but making it easy for the Japs to destroy most of them. Sailors were still sleeping on the eight battleships anchored in tandem and the many other ships there had been platted by Japanese spies and sympathizers. At the end of the two hour attack, the Japanese had lost only 19 planes. The United States lost 19 ships including all of the battleships, except for the Pennsylvania which was in dry dock, 3,457 soldiers, sailors and civilians and property damage in the millions. We did not know the total extent of our losses until a year later but everyone knew we could no longer bury our heads in the sand.

Wilburn came over and we rode around for a while and talked about what was happening and what it would mean to us and our generation. He told me, "Mary, I am going to sign up for the air force. If I have to fight I want to do it from the air and not on the ground.

I just wanted to get to myself and cry my eyes out. I knew all of the fellows my age would have to go and I couldn't stand the idea of it. I knew Jimmy would have to fight as well as lots of cousins and classmates. And I felt panicky that Wilburn would be in a plane. I knew he loved speed and really wished he could afford flying lessons but I was afraid of planes. I knew I did not have the right to try to talk him out of it. When we parted that night, I heard bells ringing but they were not joyful bells but sorrowful, sonorous bells tolling for mankind. It was all so scary.

I went to school on Monday as usual and we were convened into the auditorium to hear President Roosevelt declare war on Japan and making a promise that we would avenge the dastardly attack on our country. Young men and boys were already lining up to enlist as everyone was angry at the sneak attack on Pearl Harbor. And we were all in shock.

Wilburn picked me up at school with the news that he

had signed up to train as a naval pilot. He received his enlistment papers but had to wait for further instruction as there were no training bases as yet and it would take a little time to get geared up to start the training. So we were given a sort of reprieve.

He thought he would get to come to Pulaski during Christmas but wasn't sure. It sounded like he would be coming to see Joyce. I was going home for the holidays on Friday the 19th. I was also going to work at Harwell-Stone Dry Goods while home and was somewhat ambivalent about whether I would come back to Nashville. I think I was all mixed up at the time about my feelings. I know I was not happy to get a letter from him signed "Affectionately Yours" and not a word of love - a good ruse because it was working. Did I mention how smart he was also?

So I came home for Christmas. On Christmas Eve I was working at Harwell-Stone and Joyce was working a Kuhn's. About mid morning my brother, Jimmy, came running into the store waving a package for me. It had come in the mail. He was smiling and said, "I think it is a watch as I can hear it ticking." He and all the clerks gathered around while I unwrapped it. Sure enough, it was the prettiest little Elgin watch with a velvet band. I was so happy and proud of it since I had never had a watch.

Also I was proud for everyone to know someone thought that much of me. Of course, it was from Wilburn. I was on Cloud 9 the rest of the day. But pride comes before a fall!

At Joyce's supper break, she walked into the store. I pulled my sweater down over the watch, not wanting to hurt her. We passed a few pleasantries and I asked her, "Is Santa Claus coming to see you tonight?" With a sort of smile on her face, she pulled back her sleeve and said, "He came to see me today." Well, I couldn't resist. I pulled my sleeve back and said, "He came to see me, too." The clerks, who were aware of the tangle Joyce, Wilburn, and I were in, got a great kick out of that exchange. I hated that he sent her a watch also.

I went home that night more confused and puzzled than before. And quite deflated.

On December 26th Wilburn and Thomas came to
Pulaski. They picked me up and then we picked Joyce up
so I was Thomas' date. From a letter I have from Wilburn
written December 27th, we must have parked somewhere.
Wilburn wrote that he was glad when Thomas asked him to
drive so that he didn't have to see us so close together. I
hate myself now for treating Wilburn that way and I
remember I hated seeing Joyce by his side.

When I got home my cousin, Ann, was there to spend
the night and we slept together. She is five years older than
I am so I told her what was going on with the three of us.
She really talked to me. She told me I was crazy about
Wilburn and just wouldn't admit it. I realized she was right
and knew I had to do something about it.

In his December 27th letter, Wilburn wrote three sayings:

*"It is better to have loved and lost than to have never
loved at all."*

He told me he was grateful for all of my kindness and
sweetness and quoted:

*"Ingratitude is the rankest weed that grows, and may we
so live and act that that weed may never shed its seed in our
heart so that it grows to be a tree."*

Another quote:

*"Love really has nothing to do with Wisdom, Experience
or Logic. It is the prevailing breeze in the land of Love."*
Bruno Lessing

He closed that letter with *"Forever Yours."* I wrote a
letter back. I'm sure I tried to explain how mixed up I felt and
that I would come back to Nashville to school and we must
talk. The last letter I received from him in 1941 was in
response to my letter and written December 30th. He said
he was sorry he hurt me and he had not changed toward me
and sorry he made me feel he had. He said he loved me

very much and wanted me back in Nashville. He asked me to call as soon as I got back to Nashville and we would get everything straightened out. He said again that he loved me and would do his best to prove it to me.

I went back to Nashville, we had our talk and 1942 began a new era for us. I never doubted again that I loved him with all my heart and most of the time had no doubt of his love for me.

This ends the saga of the four months in 1941 when Wilburn and Mary were falling in love, making lots of mistakes with it, and finally came to agree that they wanted each other. Bells were finally ringing, balloons were in the sky, and the world never had seemed brighter. Love makes the world go round!

8 NEW YEAR 1942

The New Year found me back in Nashville in school still living with the Martins. But everything had changed. I WAS IN LOVE! After all the uncertainty and doubt, I was so in love I could not think straight. I had made Wilburn happy at last. We became openly a couple among his friends, but I had not met any of his family. My folks had seen Wilburn only a few times when he brought me home and went on to see Joyce. I still hesitated to tell them and so still did not want Wil to stop seeing Joyce. I was content to be just Wilburn's girl, and we did not go to Pulaski but about once in January.

Meanwhile, America was rapidly gearing up for war. Wilburn was waiting for them to call him to take his exam so he could start to fly. He could hardly wait, but I worried about being separated. Our first big disappointment was when he learned that he could not be married as long as he was a Cadet. He was unhappy about that and began planning how we could do both. He wanted to fly so badly as he had always loved speed of any kind and this was his chance to soar. But he also wanted to be married to me before we had to be separated. But there was no way I would have done anything that might have gotten him rejected for the flight training. So we were at impasse.

Every mother was worried that her sons would be called to fight. Mother Cordell (Nur) and my mother were no different. No one knew how it would affect our lives. It became urgent to love each more fervently because we never knew when our boys would be on the other side of the world.

What Wilburn and I didn't know was that Thomas had already told Joyce what was going on. But she did not let on that she even knew. Wilburn wanted to tell her and get his class pin back and hopefully his picture, but she kept writing the same as always.

In mid-February, my dad had to come to Nashville to a meeting, so Mama and my sisters came up with him. I met them in downtown Nashville and we wandered in and out of the stores and finally went to the car to wait for Daddy.

I felt it was time to confess. I told Mama that Wilburn and I were in love and thinking about getting married. She was very quiet, so I wished I had been also. My mother would have liked nothing better than for all of her children to remain single and stay at home forever.

The following week I got a call from home that they had me a job at one of the banks in Pulaski, and Jimmy was coming up to move me back home. I knew they thought if they separated Wilburn and me things would blow over. He and I were not happy over it, but it never occurred to me to question my parents. I moved back home and went to work at the Richland Bank as a bookkeeper, making $18.00 a week.

Wilburn and William Pulley came to Pulaski the last Sunday in February. I got Pulley a date with Faye Phelps and they hit it off fine. Joyce knew Wilburn was there, but he didn't see her. On February 25th he wrote me that he had received the sweetest letter from her saying that she knew he had a reason. He had hoped she would get mad and break off with him, but she didn't, so we were still unsure how to handle her. In that letter, he said he was hoping to get off the following weekend and come down as he felt we had to get everything straightened out and be able to be open with everyone that we were going to be together.

I'm sure I was writing him even more often than he wrote me, but he was not saving my letters that year. He was demanding that I write at least three times a week. The minute I said the words "I love you", he began to tell me what to do. He never stopped, but I did not mind. I loved to please him.

He was still worrying how to dump Joyce gracefully, but we could see no way to do that. He was coming down every chance he had, riding the bus some of the times and spending the weekend with us, but he did not see her. Pulaski was a small town, so she had to know what was going on. Looking back, I know I was silly to worry about her. She may have been two years younger than I but she was way ahead of me when it came to being cunning. She would have hurt me in a minute.

So far the war had not affected us. Wilburn was waiting for the government to tell him what to do and was still working nights at the Union Station terminal. My brother was trying to decide if he should wait to be drafted or enlist. All of the young men knew they were going to fight one way or the other. And everyone was worried and afraid.

And so March, 1942 came. Wilburn's March 5th letter was telling me how lonely he was since I left Nashville, how he missed me and how lost he felt. I was feeling the same way in Pulaski. Not much we could do about it.

Wilburn came to Pulaski on a Sunday (about March 8th) and we must have decided it was time to cut Joyce loose as he wrote me on March 9th that he had written to her, telling her everything and felt better.

The Naval Air Force finally began sending information as to what Wilburn would be doing. First of all, he would be sent to Clarksville, Tennessee for flight training as the bases were not ready for the influx of cadets as yet. He wanted to go ahead and get married and keep it a secret but I was holding back. I was not good at keeping secrets, especially about something so wonderful as becoming Mrs. Wilburn E. Cordell. I finally told him that we would be married at Christmas. So he decided to leave it up to me.

A nurse at the railroad who had been friendly with him was telling him goodbye. He asked her if she thought we should get married before he left. She said if we loved each other we should get married right away. That was what he wanted to hear. He really wanted us to be married. He was assuring me that he would be safe flying and that he would be careful. He was missing me more every day and I'm sure I was telling him the same thing. But things were so uncertain for everyone that plans had to be put on hold.

At that time, Wilburn's brother, John Alton, was going to school at the University of Tennessee in Knoxville. A letter on March 17th from Wilburn told me he might not get to come the following weekend as Alton was supposed to come home and he had promised him he could use his car. Wilburn had bought a car by that time so he could come to Pulaski alone. He was still waiting to hear from the Naval Air Corps and fretting over not getting his orders. He could hardly wait to start flying. I was informed that the car he bought would only go 97 mph, and he wanted one that would get up to 105 mph. I just knew he was going to get killed, and he delighted in keeping me in a tizzy over his love of speed. He didn't seem to be afraid of anything and I was afraid of everything. But I never doubted his ability to handle anything that he tackled. I was very proud of my big guy!

9 ENGAGED

Since Wilburn was so set on our being married, I agreed that we would be married at Easter instead of waiting until Christmas. He came to Pulaski the weekend of March 21st and 22nd. On the way home he blew out a tire and had to take the bus home. By that time, rubber had been rationed and it was impossible to buy anything but a used tire and they were hard to find so it was a while before his car was back on the road. It was not much of a car anyway as he had not been working long enough to afford a good one. But he wanted to be able to come to Pulaski without having to bring someone with him. But we were back to having to wait to see each other for a while.

In a letter dated March 23rd he was telling me how much he missed me, how every time he saw me it was harder for him to leave me. He said his better judgment told him we should wait, but his love told him we should grab what happiness we could in what little time we had left. He said, *"If we were married, I would know that I had you and we would have a right to be together on weekends."* I would agree to almost every proposal he made for our lives; then his good sense would kick in and he would feel that we should wait.

In a letter dated March 24th he had decided that the Easter date was not such a good idea and for me not to make plans. We would have to try to keep it a secret. And we both knew that wasn't smart. I was relieved that we would wait because I did not want to do anything that would keep him from getting to be a pilot.

I think, in looking back, we both thought too much of our parents to do what they thought we should not do. My folks had learned to love Wilburn, but his folks did not know me yet. Both sets of parents wanted us to wait. The two of us were torn in two about it, wanting to belong to each other, but wanting to do what was best. A letter from Wilburn on March 25th was telling me all the reasons we should wait. So I tried to settle down to waiting.

Meanwhile the rumor got out in Pulaski as well as Nashville that we were married and I had to fend off all kind of questions. Wilburn was having the same problem. We found out later that Joyce and Thomas had been the source of that misinformation.

By this time America was in full war mode. Young men 18 and over had to register for the draft. They were leaving in droves. Their numbers would come up and when a group from this area was ready to go, the Army would send a truck for them and haul them off like cattle. Everyone would go to the Square to see them off. There was much hugging and oceans of tears. But no one complained. We all knew we had to fight the enemy. President Roosevelt was everyone's hero. Though he led us from a wheelchair, he was a strong and courageous leader. At our house, we were sad because we knew Jimmy would soon have to go. Like Wilburn, he did not want the Army so he joined the Marine Corps.

So the first week of April, 1942 found Wilburn and I still tossing around the desire to be together and knowing it was not possible at that time. He was having trouble finding what was needed to get his car up and going again. The government had frozen rubber and anything else that would be required for the war effort. Gasoline was soon rationed but that was not due to lack of fuel but to save on wear and tear of our cars. It was not too long until groceries were rationed also. We had to have a ration stamp for almost everything you ate except what was raised in our garden and truck patches.

Life was full of ups and downs, doubts and uncertainties. There was such a flurry of activity everywhere due to the war effort. Here in Pulaski, we copied what the larger cities were doing and set up a chapter of the USO. That was for the entertainment and housing of soldiers who would come into the towns and cities for weekends. We maintained a couple of bedrooms right off the Square so that the soldiers who came for the weekend could have a place to sleep. We did not entertain them with dances and parties as did the larger cities but they came here anyway. We had repeat weekenders and I met several nice boys. We always had breakfast for them. When they left, we cleaned the rooms for the next visitors. Wilburn was not too happy that I was into that but we all had to do our part. The boys were usually a long way from home.

The April 13, 1942 letter from Wilburn was a very sweet love letter. I always thought I was the one who gave the most of myself and my feelings but after reading the letters so many, many years after they were written, I'm not sure. He was worried that I wanted us to break up, but he said, *"I will not let you go very easily. I am going to love you always if you will let me"*. He had not been able to come down in at least two weeks. It was very frustrating.

I was still working at the Richland Bank and living at home. I had my picture made for Wilburn and he promised to have one made for me. He was still working at the railroad and waiting for his call to duty. The car still was not road ready so he very graciously gave me permission to go out with other boys if I would be good but only until he could come down here. As if I could look at anyone else and he knew it!

So my birthday came. I was not enjoying it very much as I wanted to share it with Wilburn and he still had no wheels as far as I knew. We lived on the corner of Fifth Street and Highway 64 and were sitting on the front porch late that Friday afternoon. We had three or four ladies from the community visiting with us. I was bored and lost in my own thoughts. It was my 19th birthday.

Suddenly a strange car turned the corner on what

seemed like two wheels and came to a halt at our house. I looked and it was Wilburn. He had just traded for another car and he had made it for my birthday. I knew he would never get out with such a crowd of women on the porch, so I bounced down the steps and got in the car with him. We sat and talked, trying to not touch each other in front of everyone. I wanted to hug him so badly. Without any ado he tossed a small box into my lap. I opened it and it was a small diamond ring. We were legally engaged at last. It was the prettiest thing I had ever seen and I jumped out of the car and ran up the steps to show it off to everyone. Then with Mama's permission, I bounced back down and joined Wilburn and we went for a long ride. It was the best birthday I could have had. And we were finally engaged. Balloons were in the sky, bells were ringing everywhere and I was happy enough to burst.

10 MEETING THE CORDELLS

I was so excited over getting my ring, I could hardly sleep. Wil and I came back from our ride and he spent the night with us. By that time, my folks had pretty well accepted the fact that Wil would be a part of our family. The sisters adored him, and he and James, my brother, hit it off right away. I guess he had to share a bedroom with James when he came for overnight.

I got the sweetest love letter from him, written April 29, 1942. He was telling me what a good time he had over the weekend but that he wasn't going to infringe on my folks when he came from now on. But we always won out and he stayed at our house (hotel accommodations in Pulaski were not very plentiful). He also said in that letter that he did not think he could ever make me believe how much he loved me. Also he was ready to get married any time I wanted to. I really wanted us to set a date, but there was still the problem of his being kicked out of the Air Corps if they found out he was married. The government wanted only single pilots because of the dangers involved in flying. Single men would be more daring.

Those were the days of love and roses. I literally walked on air. I was so proud of my little diamond and prouder still of my big guy.

Wil had a sister three years younger than he so his parents were still involved in high school affairs. On April 30, 1942, Wil wrote that they had gone to Central High School

with Elizabeth Ann (Pansy) that night to see a Senior play.
In this letter he informed me that I was the sweetest girl in
the world. He wanted me to come to Nashville the weekend
of Mother's Day because his family would be together and
his buddies were having a picnic. I hated to be gone on
Mother's Day but my mother agreed that I should go and
meet Wil's family so I told him I would come.

I must have not been well at this time because he
wrote:

*"Darling, I hope you are much better now. If
anything happened to you I know I'd be ready to give up.
You're about all the enjoyment I have. So please take
good care of yourself. After all, I have quite some
interest in you."*

(I imagine I was just lovesick and not eating right.)
Wil's friend, William Pulley, had really fallen for my
friend, Faye Phelps. So the two of them came to Pulaski the
weekend before Mother's Day and Pulley wanted Faye to
come to the picnic the next Sunday, but she wasn't sure
about it.

Wil was wondering if I really wanted to get married. He
said when he read my letters he thought I did, but when we
were together I changed completely. We had made up our
minds to get something settled when he came, but then we
didn't settle anything. I never wavered from wanting to
marry him, but I just knew it wasn't the smartest thing for us
to do when our world was tipping on its axis, so to speak,
and no one knew what to plan on.

Hardly anyone was idle those days. America was
turning out war supplies daily, building planes, ships and
Army vehicles. Women went to work in factories all over the
country. Pulaski had a General Shoe Factory and it was
immediately geared up to turn out Army boots. I was still
working as a bookkeeper at Richland Bank using a hand-
cranked machine to post the accounts. Tootsie Cole (later
McCord) was the other bookkeeper. We stayed close
friends all of our lives and still are. Parmenas Cox was

President of Richland Bank and Robert E. Curry was a Teller. Both of them became officers of the First National Bank in later years.

Something I had said or done or not done made Wil tell me that he was not going to mention getting married any more. I think he knew also that we should wait. That letter was written on May 5, 1942.

On May 6th he wrote again. He was hoping that Faye would not want to make the trip with us to Nashville because he wanted the day for just the two of us. He had bought another car by then, a cute little coupe with a rather cramped back seat. He said if Faye wanted to come to Nashville he would make her welcome.

Mother's Day arrived. Faye decided not to go to Nashville. James and Bill Maultsby wanted to go to Nashville to spend the day. They knew their days of Freedom were running out and they would be off to war. Wil had to work Saturday night but he came down directly from getting off from work on Sunday morning. I asked him if James and Bill could ride up with us. He was happy to have them, so they crowded into the little back seat. Wil drove so fast going to Nashville that when we took the boys to downtown and let them out Bill asked James, "Do you think he didn't want us to ride with them?" James replied, "No, he was just making sure we don't go back with them tonight." Sure enough, they rode the bus home.

We had to go by the Cordells then for Wil to get cleaned up. I met Mother Cordell (Nur), Gram and Elizabeth Ann (Pansy). We went to church and then to Lawrence and Myrtle's house for Sunday dinner. So I finally met my other family. And fell in love with all of them. There were Evelyn, Wil's older sister, her husband Allen and Denny, their five year old son; Lawrence, Wil's oldest brother, his wife Myrtle, their three year old son Lawrence, Jr. ;Clifford, Wil's second brother, his wife Elizabeth, their children Wayne and Bobbi Jean; Nur and Gram, Pansy and Nur's sister, Auntie and her husband, Horace. I guess his other brother, John Alton, was in Knoxville at college, as I do not recall his being there. I just loved all of them, especially the children. They were all so cute and sweet. I felt like I had known them all of my life. I still love the Cordells.

We did go to the picnic but stayed only long enough to let them know we were not being snooty. Then we headed back to Pulaski because I had to go to work the next morning and Wil had to work that night.

How on earth had I attracted that dynamic man? I was always a worrier, a scaredy cat, wanting guarantees before taking a chance on everything I wanted to do. He was courageous, afraid of nothing and no one. He thought he could conquer anything or anyone and you know, I thought he could too. He frightened everyone who rode with him with his fast driving, but he never had a wreck. He concentrated on what he was doing. I wore my legs out putting on brakes when I rode with him. It never occurred to me that he would let me get hurt and he didn't.

I guess we forgot our vow not to talk about getting married because his letter of May 12th was full of it. He got back home that weekend and told everyone we got married. In fact we were planning on doing so. Thomas and Sarah wanted to get married as well, so we were all four making plans. But Wilburn told me again not to tell anyone unless I wanted to talk to my mother. I didn't because I knew she would discourage it. I was happy and I felt secure about planning to belong to Wil Cordell, especially after meeting his family.

Oh, yeah, the bells were really ringing and I loved every moment of that April and May and looked forward to balloons in the sky and nothing but happy days for the coming summer.

A letter on May 13th was a sweet love letter, still talking about getting married. He was having a hard time convincing everyone we had not married when he said we did. He loved to kid people. He wanted us to be married first and tell his folks after the deed was done. I felt the same way about telling Mama and Daddy. How young and naïve the two of us were those days. We had no inkling that a monkey wrench was going to soon be thrown in the way of the best laid plans.

11 ACCEPTANCE TO NAVAL AIR CORPS

Wilburn and Thomas came to Pulaski on May 18th. As soon as he got home that night, he wrote me a letter to say that I should not say anything about getting married to anyone until we had a chance to talk. He said a letter had come that day that changed everything and he did not want to write about it but wanted to see me face to face. He was still hoping I would not change my mind about marrying after our talk. He told me he would never deceive me, he did not drink or see other girls. I was the only one he would ever love. I worried and wondered about the letter he had received.

He came on Saturday, May 22nd and stayed overnight. The letter he had was an acceptance to the Naval Air Corps. All that was left to do was to get his birth certificate, his Dad's signature on some papers and then he would go to Atlanta for exams. Then he could start to fly. We both agreed to put off any wedding plans and give him the chance to fly as it was his dream. A new way of life began. And time seemed to pass on sluggish feet.

In May the government was gearing up to draft men 18 and over so the young men were trying to get into their favorite service branch before being drafted into the Army. Wil was anxiously waiting for the Navy to let him know when to report to Atlanta for entrance exams. James and Whitfield

McCracken went to Nashville to join the Marines. They were twenty at the time. Bill Maultsby, their close buddy, was a year or so younger and could have waited, but when he found out they had signed up, he went to Nashville the next day and enlisted to go into the Marines with them. So the reality of War was settling in and no one was exempt from worry of some kind or another.

I really had a great fear of Wil flying. He was always trying to persuade me to be happy that he would be a pilot. But he was such a dare-devil that I was really afraid he would take chances. His love of speed won out, so I accepted his choice.

On May 27th he wrote that he would go to Atlanta the next day. I guess I had written him that everyone was telling me he had joined the Naval Air Force to keep from marrying me. He said I could just marry him before he left and prove them wrong. He said that should prove that he really wanted me. But of course, he knew I would not marry him and ruin his chance to fly. I knew flying was his second love and I guess I was jealous of it.

In the May 27th letter he told me John Alton was coming home the next day so Nur was happy. I guess he was out of school for the summer. Wilburn wanted him to go into the Navy with him but his eyes were not good enough. Besides, he did not share Wilburn's love of speed and did not like airplanes. This letter was real sweet. He was assuring me that I would keep house for him some day and he would never change toward me. He gave me his word. So I had to be content with that.

The first letter that Wilburn saved from me was written on Sunday, May 31, 1942. My last letter from him had been written May 27th and I was expecting him to come down to Pulaski on Sunday. I wrote that I looked for him all day and he had not even called me. So I was worried (as usual) but we had company. Bro. Fox and his family had come to Pulaski and I had helped entertain his 16 year old son.

James and his two buddies had left for the Marines so there wasn't much to be happy about. I was telling Wilburn that my aunt, Aunt Mabel, was being operated on for cancer the next day and Mama and Daddy were going, leaving me and Paula in charge of everything. Also Grandpa Whitlock was sick in bed; Aunt Birtie Lee had been burned in El Dorado, Arkansas when a gas stove had blown up. So we were thinking we might have to get James home due to all the emergencies. Hindsight proves that everything got better except Aunt Mabel. She was never well any more before she died. I wound up the letter wondering how he did in Atlanta and gently chastising him for not letting me hear from him as he had promised to come down that day.

But bells still rung when I heard his name called, stars twinkled brightly when I saw him come in sight and I was drowning in love for him. And so we made it to June, 1942.

12 WARTIME 1942

And so we reached June 1942 with a letter from Wil telling me why he had not been able to come the Sunday before. He had gotten in from Atlanta, tired out, and had to go to work that night and just had to get some sleep on Sunday. The exams in Atlanta had been very stressful. Only four out of the 27 passed. He was really proud of himself for being one of the four. I was proud, also. He was modest and said he guessed he was just luckier than those that failed. But I knew he was just a little smarter...maybe not just a little.

I finally called him on Tuesday, June 2. It was a rare thing to make a long distance call back then and we only made them in emergencies. But I called. I do not recall the exact conversation but I guess I was fussing because he had disappointed me on Sunday and left me wondering how things went in Atlanta. He was so sorry. He had not realized just how unthinking it was until I called. He said he could not go back to sleep for two hours just thinking about it.

Wil could go on the offensive if I was upset about something he had done, and it always worked because I would wind up trying to pacify him. He told me in the letter of June 2nd that he had seen all of the letters John Al's girlfriend, Elizabeth (Becky) Frost, had written and some of them were four or five pages long. So he guessed Becky just loved John Al more than I loved him because my letters were not that long. When I wrote him next the letter was five pages long. He did tell me before closing the letter that he loved me very much, more than he could ever tell me. He said he knew he acted like he did not care lots of times but he really did love me more than anything else. That was all it took to get back in my good graces.

He also wrote that he would tell me what the Commanding Officer in Atlanta said about me. I cannot remember if he ever told me, but I feel sure it was something to do with my refusing to marry him and keep him from getting his wings. He also wrote that Nur (his mother) said to tell me she would not have awakened him to talk to anyone else but me. I always felt Wil's family loved me.

By June the War was beginning in earnest for America. And so many other things were happening.   On February 10th, the world's fastest ocean liner, France's S. S. Normandie was gutted by fire and it sank in the New York harbor. That was quite a loss for the Allies.

On February 19th of 1942, President Roosevelt signed the order that allowed the military to move 112,000 Japanese-Americans from their homes into concentration camps. That was sad because some of them were born in America, and some fought against Japan. But it was hard to know friend from foe, and most Americans were really angry at anything that even looked Japanese. So it was partly for their protection.

General Douglas MacArthur, fighting on Bataan, was ordered by President Roosevelt to leave the Philippines to go to Australia to take charge of the Southwest Pacific forces. He traveled by submarine to Australia. All of our information was mostly gained by going to the movie theatres and watching the news on the movie screen. No TV, no computers, no means of transferring pictures to the general public so we all had to use our imaginations and die a thousand deaths while waiting to hear from our boys.

On April 10th, 1942, the Bataan Death March began. The Japanese forced 10,000 U. S. prisoners-of-war and about

45,000 Filipino scouts to march 120 miles to San Fernando. All the sick and wounded who were unable to march at the end of the day were shot, stabbed or buried alive. With only one meal of rice a day and no water, over 5200 Americans and thousands of Filipinos died in the 6-day long ordeal. In the first two months of stockade life, 2200 more American prisoners and 27,000 Filipinos died due to mistreatment, malnutrition and cold-blooded murder. At least the Japanese-Americans in U. S. concentration camps were well fed, housed and clothed, and allowed to socialize within the camp.

The first offensive strike on Japanese soil occurred April 18th, 1942 when Col. James Doolittle's carrier-based flyers bombed Tokyo. It was a one-way trip for the fighters. They tried to reach China after dropping their bombs and either bailed out or tried to crash on Chinese soil.

May 3-8, 1942, was a milestone battle in the Coral Sea. It was a showdown battle fought exclusively by carrier-based aircraft. The surface ships were 180 miles apart and were never fired on. This battle, led by Adm. Frank Fletcher, disrupted Japanese high command plans to invade Australia. Initially, Fletcher sank the light carrier, Shoho, which deprived the Japanese troop ships of their air cover. So Japanese Vice Admiral Inouye ordered the troop ships to turn around. Meanwhile, two Japanese carriers, Auikaka and Shokaku, had located Fletcher's carriers, USS Yorktown and USS Lexington. Fletcher had no time to rearm his planes for a fresh attack, but he was aided by bad weather to save his carriers from the 29 Japanese bombers sent to find them. In spite of the heavy rain, Fletcher sent fighters up, and they shot down most of the 29 bombers. On May 8, the decisive air battle was fought. Fletcher lost 33 planes and the Japanese 43. The USS Lexington was badly damaged and had to be scuttled. But America had won a decisive battle.

By May, 1942, America had built and delivered to the troops 67 escort vessels and a second "60 vessels in 60 days "effort was begun. We needed armed ships on both sides of our continent. Submarines were a real threat to our

Atlantic seaboard. By May 15th gasoline was rationed. We were allowed three gallons a week to cover ordinary driving demands. Ration books were issued making travel almost impossible. It was considered unpatriotic to drive anywhere if it was close enough to walk. Wil and I knew he was not going to be able to come to see me so he sold his car. When he could come, he rode the bus.

Shortly after the Coral Sea Battle there was another milestone battle at Midway in the Pacific. Using Midway Island as a base, the U. S. was able to stop Japanese Admiral Yamamoto's thrust into the South Pacific. He lost four carriers, two cruisers, and 11 other vessels. He kept to his quarters, so we heard, during the retreat into Japanese home waters as he considered himself to be in disgrace. He was the Japanese admiral, who after Pearl Harbor, made the statement, "We have awakened a sleeping tiger". And he was right. Americans were angry and determined.

We got our news from the newspapers or radio and short newsreels at the movies. News was already old by the time we got it, but even I knew how much the Pacific War depended on air power.

There was always the hope that the war would be over before James or Wil got out of training. Malcolm and Howard, my cousins, were already in the Army.   John Alton got his draft papers. He went in as a conscientious objector and was assigned to the Medical Corps. He was in Europe a long time, and except for not carrying a gun, served his time as valiantly as any gun-carrying soldier.

The summer of 1942 was so scary to all of us but we all pitched in and did not complain. Instead of bells ringing for me, I heard patriotic music and marching bands and instead of stars shooting across my sky, I saw bullets and cannons and planes bursting into flames and spent a lot of time with God in prayer. Our dependence on God was such a consolation in those trying times and He did not let us down.

13 JUNE 1942

On June 7, 1942, Wilburn wrote that he was still in limbo as to when he would be called back to Atlanta to be sworn in. There was some mix-up about paperwork in Nashville; he was certainly ready go. He had an argument with his boss at the railroad and told his boss to "Go to Hell", so he did not know if he would still have a job. His Dad told him to resign and then go back to work for the railroad after the war. He thought he would do that. In this letter he was telling me how much he missed me after I had left Nashville. No more than I missed him, I'm sure. Love is such sweet sorrow. The emotions of being in love were so varied and so intense. For me, loving Wilburn was all I could think about night and day.

June 10, Wilburn wrote that Nashville had their first blackout. It lasted from 9 to 9:30 PM. I guess it was a practice run. Things could really be dark and scary at night during a blackout. The sirens would go off, and then all the lights would go off. Shades and draperies were drawn so not a beam of light could be seen from the air. We went to basements or designated safe places and waited until the lights came back. America was so blessed that we were never attacked on our own soil, other than Hawaii.

Back to Wilburn and Mary. On June 12, Wilburn went to Atlanta again, and on June 13, Saturday, he was sworn into the U. S. Naval Air Corps. He was scheduled to be subject to 24 hour call and would have to report to Athens, Georgia. But he felt sure it would be August before he had to go to Athens. He started Civilian Pilot Training that next week or so. He would be at Austin Peay in Clarksville, Tennessee, until further orders. He was wishing James would try to go with him. All the boys who were going with him that he knew had flunked out. He wrote that John Alton had to go to the Draft Board the next day to be examined. So Mother Cordell was really upset that they both would be leaving. He also wrote that he got homesick the two days he was in Atlanta. He did not know what he would do when he was gone for a long time. This letter was written June 14, 1942.

His letter of June 17th was written the day after he came down to see me on Tuesday night. He was planning to come back on Thursday because he planned to go back to work for the railroad on Friday. The following is a verbatim quote from that letter:

> "Darling, I didn't tell you last night but you never looked more beautiful to me than last night. I don't know whether it was because I had not seen you in so long or what it was but you sure looked good to me. And you acted like you might love me but I can't help but doubt it when you keep refusing what I want most. (He still wanted to get married.)
> But perhaps you are right in refusing but I guess when you love anyone as I love you, you don't think of anything else but that. What's right or what's wrong doesn't seem to matter. Regardless of what you do, I guess I'll just keep loving you and hoping. You can't keep me from doing that. Nothing can change that."

I want it understood that Wilburn never once asked me to do anything that would have been wrong for us to do. He just wanted to be married. As for my being beautiful, "Love is blind" and "Beauty is in the eye of the Beholder" would apply.

He also wrote in the above mentioned letter that he

stayed with Donald one night in Atlanta. He wore one of Donald's uniforms and they went to downtown Atlanta. They had a good time but spent most of it dodging MPs because Wilburn had on white shoes. He loved to be daring like that.

He did not get to come to Pulaski on the 18th after all. He must have called me as his next letter does not say why. But he did come on Sunday, the 21st, and I think that was the Sunday afternoon we took a quilt and radio and spent the afternoon at Bevills Springs. That was a picnic area in the country. The spring water was wonderful. We listened to Sammy Kaye and his band and just lounged in the shade talking and planning. We must have resurrected the idea of going ahead and getting married.

Another quote:

"Well, darling, I haven't changed my mind about marrying. You said when I left you that I would change, but I only want it worse. I sure hope you will see it my way. You will try to, won't you, darling? Please."

He had to come by bus that day so he said he was late getting home. Mother Cordell was waiting up for him. She was such a lovely, loving person.

Apparently he did not call me the Thursday he was supposed to come down. I found out later that Donald had been home for a few days and I always felt Donald was a bad influence on Wilburn. So I guess I was upset with him when he came on Sunday. The letter of June 23rd was trying to make up for not calling me. Also, I had written him a letter that he received on Tuesday, the 23rd, and I guess I said "NO" to getting married before he left. I quote again:

"I have been thinking of you every minute of this week. I guess I'm pretty lonesome, too. In fact, I know I am. And getting your letter saying "NO" sure didn't do me any good either. I didn't mean to say anymore about it but I will say this and then we will forget about it for good. You said "NO" and if that is

*what you want that is what you shall have. Even
though I still want you very much I cannot force you to
marry me. But if you ever change your mind, darling,
I guess I will still be waiting. If something does
happen and we are sorry that we didn't marry, don't
forget. I have given you every chance."*

I know I must have been miserable all of this time, not
being able to marry Wilburn and be happy, but knowing that
if I did and he got kicked out of the Air Force, he would never
forgive me. So I called myself being sensible. And too, the
War was on everyone's mind. The future seemed so
uncertain.

14 JUNE & JULY 1942

On June 24, 1942, Wilburn wrote that John Alton got his Classification Card on that day. He was classified as 1-A. Wilburn was quite upset that John Alton was going to let the Army draft him. He was so smart that Wilburn felt he could try for Officer School or something. But I guess Alton knew what he wanted. And that was just to be a Medic and not carry a gun. Wilburn also wrote in that letter that Donald's leave was about up and he felt they would not see each other for two or three more years. True to his word, there was no pressure on me to get me to change my mind about getting married.

I guess I must have written Wilburn that week and asked him to leave Donald alone. He wrote that he knew I wanted him to leave all of the boys he ran around with alone. I knew they drank a lot and drove too fast. I was afraid they might influence my big guy to drink and that was the one thing I could never live with. He said he couldn't just drop them as they had been friends forever. He had a mind of his own and he promised me that he would not drink with them. So I had to be content with that. He told me to forget about Sunday night as we did not do anything to be ashamed of. I cannot remember what he was talking about but I know now we never did anything to hide from anyone. I had just been raised by such a strict mother that I thought any bodily contact was wrong. How times have changed!

In a letter of June 26th he was telling me about seeing a boy who had gone into the Army Air Corps. The boy was very happy about everything so Wilburn was wishing they would call him up. He said if they didn't soon do something that he might just try to get into the Army Air Corps rather the Navy. He couldn't wait to fly and was still working nights at the railroad.

He did not come down the weekend of the 27th, and wrote me again on Sunday night the 28th. He was supposed to have gone on a picnic with Thomas and Sarah but when he found out they had him a date he would not go. It always seemed to me that Thomas would just as soon see us break up. But by that time it was too late.

Donald had left that Sunday, but he was wishing he had gotten married while on furlough. His girl was named Hilda. I think she felt about Wilburn as I did about Donald, and I never got to know her at all, even after the War when they were married and lived in Nashville. The old gang just drifted apart.

Wil (I had shortened his name by then) wrote again on the 30h answering a letter I had written. I must have told him that I started to go out with someone else when he didn't come. He wrote:

"It's a good thing for you that you didn't go off with any boy. That means before I leave and after too. And don't forget it."

I had no intention of doing that anyway.

So that was the first six months of 1942. James, Whitfield Mcracken and Bill Maultsby were in the Marines by that time. James was training to be a navigator. They had come through a rough boot camp or probably were still in training at this time. I think they were at Quantico Marine Base in Virginia. Alton was poised to leave any time. Wil had been sworn into the Naval Air Corps, but the delay in calling him had him threatening to transfer to the Army. It was not the happiest of times for me. I was working at the bank, posting on a table size hand-operated posting machine. I just sat all day feeding it figures. I think I worked every Saturday at Harwell-Stone Dry Goods or Sunshine Cleaners, whichever one needed me. But I wanted to be more useful in the War effort and I wanted to be with Wil.

On Sunday, July 5th, we were still not together. He had let Alton have his car because Alton did not have much time left. He said he had had a hard night at work the night before and that everyone thought he was crazy to be working before he left. He said he didn't want to quit until he had to. I think the fight with the boss was just overlooked. He was telling me that his aunt from Smyrna had asked what he was going to do with his wife when he left. He said that they did not have to operate on his brother. I do not remember if that was Lawrence or Clifford. Also one of the babies had been sick. I do not remember if that was Lawrence, Jr. or Bobbi Jean. At that time there were only four children in the family - Denny, Wayne, Lawrence, Jr. and Bobbi Jean.

Wil got his call to duty. He wrote me on July 7, 1942. He was just settling in at Austin Peay in Clarksville, TN. He said there was not much to do there. He and his roommate, Hubert, went to a dance at the girls' dorm but did not stay long. Wil did not care much for dancing. That was fine with me as I was never allowed to dance. He said they just left and went to a movie. That was everyone's entertainment during those years. You could go to a movie and have popcorn for a quarter. And that was where we got all of our war news from - the newsreels.

Wil was happy at last as he knew he would soon be able to sprout wings and soar. A letter the first day said they would start classes the first day. Their schedule, until they could begin flying, would be physics from 1:30 to 3 PM, athletics until 5 PM, supper at 5:30, and then math at 7 PM. He said he left his mother crying so he had to write to her.

A letter squeezed in between classes on July 8 said it was so hot when they had athletics. No one had air conditioning. I had sent him a picture before he left home. He may have been making fun but he wrote:

Mary W. Cordell

> *"I just had a very nice compliment on your picture. A boy across the hall came in and wanted to know what movie star that was. I told him it was my girl, and he just laughed and said, "There isn't any boy up here good looking enough to have a girl like that. "*

Jokes aside, it sounded like music to my ears. Oh, I loved that man!

15 FINALLY FLYING

Wil promised to have a picture made for me as soon as he could. I wanted one before they made him cut his beautiful wavy hair. The War had finally hit home. I and everyone else was missing someone very much and we all lived in terrible dread of a phone call or an officer of some kind showing up at our door to tell us we had lost our loved one. All we could do was pray and hope for the best and to write letters to every service man we knew to try to keep his spirits up. Wil was pushing me to write two or three times a day as everyone else had multiple girlfriends and he had only me to hear from. I tried very hard to do everything he asked me to.

He was in Nashville the weekend of July 12 but he did not make it to Pulaski. He had sold his car to William Pulley. Alton had gotten his orders to leave July 21. Mother Cordell was very distraught over everything. All of the family were coming to her house that night so Wilburn thought that would cheer her up.

On July 13, he wrote a very short and unsatisfactory letter - mostly to fuss at me because he did not get a letter from me that day. He said he started flying that date and really liked it. Several of the boys did not like it. I was glad he was happy to finally be in the air but I was very uneasy about it. He apologized for being upset over not getting a letter from me on Monday because he got two on Tuesday.

He was talking about James leaving and how he wished he could have seen him again before he left. He wrote,"

"Don't worry, darling. He will be back."

We could not be sure of that as we were hearing of casualties every day. Wil said they were going solid thirteen hours a day. Said he did not have time for lunch that day, July 14th. He said they were experimenting with them to see just how much a boy could take. So far, they were doing okay, but they kept adding new things every day.

A letter written July 17 was telling me that Lt. Col. Outlaw, for whom the airfield was named, was killed that week. They had closed the airfield for two days in his honor. So they were behind on flying and he would probably not get to come to see me that weekend. But he did get to come on Sunday, July 19th.

The next day, he wrote:

"Darling, I don't think I have ever enjoyed a day more than I did yesterday. It is just the hopes of more Sundays like that that keep me going."

They had really had a hard day. He said all of the instructors were mad because so many cut their classes on Saturday and they were threatening to fix it where they could not leave at all on weekends. So he was feeling like telling them where to go, but he said:

"I can't. I have just got to make good at this. If I don't then I don't care what happens. I have looked forward to this for practically all of my life and then to make a failure would be the worst thing I could do."

I had to accept that, for Wil, flying was a must. I also had to accept that his love of it was the only rival I had. And yet I prayed fervently that he would succeed in completing his training.

He wrote a second letter on the same day and it was a

sweet love letter. He had two tests that day and just knew he failed both of them. He said he guessed he would have to go back to his high school habits where the less he studied, the better grades he made. He always expected to fail, but he never did. He did say that he had his best day of flying that day. In this letter, he was recalling the night in December 1941 when I had told him I loved him and he went home and called me and we talked for over an hour.

"Do you remember? I will never forget. We can't afford to forget what time we have had together. That is just about all we have, just a handful of memories. We do not have too many unhappy memories, do we? We have gotten along better, far better than the average couple. But it takes faults in both people to start an argument, since I do not know of any major faults you have, I suppose we are fairly safe. I guess I have enough faults for both of us. I know one great fault I have, and that is loving you too much. If something were to come between us then I would be lost, because I don't feel like I am working just for my future but for both of us. I hope you feel the same way. I know I am not much to put your future in but I promise you I will do my best."

So many of our few times together were spent with family. Daddy would sometimes let us have the car, but we did a lot of our courting in our living room. My sister, Nancye, was only five but she loved to be right under our feet. I guess Wil had really gotten there late Saturday that weekend. I remember we were in the living room and Nancye was lying on the floor with her feet between Wil and me. I kept trying to persuade her to go play or something. The little prissy thing said, "No. I'm going to stay and see if he kisses you." I wanted to throttle her. Wil wrote in the next letter:

"Don't let Nancye see too much. Ha!"

He loved my sisters almost as much as I did. He always knew if he got me he got my sisters also.

16 SOLO FLIGHT

Apparently we had not had word from James yet as to where he would be training, so we had no address. Wilburn was assuring me in his letter of July 22nd that James would be fine even though he was in the toughest branch of the service - the Marines. Wil said he would not drop out if he could. He was almost ready to solo, and that worried me. He wrote in that letter:

"Remember you told me if I couldn't think of anything to write about to just write 'I love you' ten times. Well, I won't write it ten times but I mean it as much as if I said it a hundred times. So goodnight, darling."

His letters kept me going through those sad and fearful days.

The letter on July 23rd was pretty short. But at the end, he wrote:

"Well, 1. I love you, 2. I love you, 3. I love you, 4. I love you, 5. I love you, 6. I love you, 7. I love you, 8. I love you, 9. I love you, 10. I love you."

He was a mess. It was already A Love So Dear and more to come, we hoped.

On July 26 Wil wrote that he finally had a picture made for me, but he did not like it at all. He wanted me to see the small one before he had the larger one made. I loved the picture, so he went ahead and had the large one made. He wanted me to send another one, and I did. Pictures were important when you couldn't see the real thing. He also told me that Alton would be leaving for a base somewhere on August 5th, so he had to go to Nashville the next Sunday regardless.

He was all upset when he wrote on Monday, July 27th. He said it had been a blue Monday when nothing had gone right. His flying was the worst he had done, and he was behind in all of his lessons. And there was no letter from me, and he was sure I was too busy doing something else over the weekend to write to him. Evelyn and Elizabeth Ann (Pansy), his sisters, and some friends had come to see him on Sunday but he had gone to the airport and missed them. He really needed some TLC, and I was not there to comfort him.

His letter of July 28th was much better. He had had a good day and did some of his best flying. He didn't say but I'm sure he got a letter or two from me that day, or I would have heard about it loud and clear. He said they had a Navy instructor there that day who talked to them about an hour and answered their questions. He told them that only 2 or 3 out of their whole class would finish. They could consider themselves miracle men if they finished with only a high school education. Wil was not giving up. He ended that letter trying to make up for fussing at me the day before.

"Well, darling, I miss you more every day, if that is possible. I sometimes wonder why I didn't listen to you and stay out of this. But I guess it is best this way. So let's make the best of it. Well, I'll close now. Goodnite, darling, and any time I say or do anything to hurt you, please overlook it because I do not mean it."

His letter of July 29th was upbeat. He said he had a

card from Elizabeth Ann wanting him to be sure to come home that weekend for John Alton's send-off. But he was afraid it would be late Saturday night before he could get there.

His letter of July 30th was one of contained excitement.

"Well, darling, it's all over now. You can stop worrying. I SOLOED TODAY". But I tell you it sure made me feel funny to be up there by myself. The instructor went out to take off with me and just as I started to take off he said, "Well, here's where I get out!" I wasn't afraid but I did feel a little different. He told me to fly around the field and land three times. When I got through he told me it was perfect and that made him about as happy as it did me, because he was afraid I would crack up. All this is just one small step in the future. There are still many hours of hard work between me and my Wings. But it still makes you feel better to know you have soloed."

He said he needed to write to James. I was always so happy he and James hit it off so well. James was still in training and Wil was on his way to being a pilot in the Navy or Marines and I was still in Pulaski, at home, working at the bank, and missing him so much.

Wil did get home that Saturday night. Mother Cordell had invited me to come for the weekend. Was he surprised to find me there!! It was a wonderful weekend, yet sad because John Alton was leaving. The whole Cordell family came and went as well as some of the Lawrence kin. I loved being with the Cordell family. Pansy and I became close friends early on in spite of the difference in our ages. She was still in high school.

Wil was so quiet and subdued that weekend, but he explained in the next letter that he just could not be cheerful for wondering when, if ever, he and John Alton would be at home together again. It was a hard time for everyone, but I knew Wil was glad I was there. That Sunday was August 2, 1942.

A letter written when he got back to Clarksville that night

told me he was already missing me, and it had only been two hours since we parted at the bus station.

"Maybe after being apart for a few more years, we'll get used to it. I guess I will always miss you, darling, but I suppose that is what love is. I love you more than I could ever try to tell you. It's another one of our few weekends gone but not forgotten. I say that, darling, because I will always remember it. If we didn't have that much we would not have anything at all, would we?"

I cherished his letters, read them over and over and wrote to
him every day. I know my letters were full of love because I lived and breathed with him in my heart. Love was such exquisite torture at times!

17 AUGUST 1942

Wil had his final math exam on August 4, 1942. He felt sure he made pretty good on it. It had rained all week, and they would have to make up flying on Sunday. He hoped he could come to Pulaski the next Saturday:

"I'm glad that you enjoyed this weekend. I really did. I don't know of anything that would have made this weekend any more complete for me. I almost fell over when I saw you. But it was about the most pleasant surprise I've ever had. Mother had never invited any of my girl friends to their house. I hope you will try to go up to see them every chance you get."

August 6th was Election Day in most of the Tennessee counties. My Dad ran for County Clerk that year, but in Pulaski, politics at that time was run by a handful of people in the county. They were called "The Machine". Unless you were running for The Machine, you never got elected. Daddy lost but it was a good experience for the whole family because we all electioneered. Most businesses had a holiday . I was off and remember passing out Daddy's cards all day.

Wil wrote that a Navy inspector had been there. He told them they would be through in Clarksville by September 1st.

Then they would get 3 or 4 weeks furlough before going to pre-flight school and officer training. I was praying for delays so maybe Wil and James and John Alton, as well as lots of cousins and friends would never make it to the battlefields. That was wishful thinking!

The war was gaining momentum. We were fighting on both sides of the world. Russia and U. S. left-wing elements were clamoring for a "2nd Front" so Roosevelt and Churchill executed "Operation Torch". This plan called for an invasion of French North Africa, then using it for a jump-off stage into Sicily and Italy.

On August 7th, a milestone battle was begun on Guadalcanal in the Pacific. There were six months of jungle fighting on that island. It was 2500 square miles. General Vandergrift's 16,000 Marines, supported by Army elements, forced veteran Japanese troops to retreat. The General began the vicious battle under a severe handicap. On August 9, 1942, Japanese cruisers and destroyers surprised Admiral Turner's task force off Saro Island at night. They sank three heavy U. S. cruisers and the Australian cruiser CANBERRA. But the Japanese commander did not follow up on his opportunity to attack U. S. transport ships still being unloaded for the Marine landing at Guadalcanal. Admiral Fletcher, having suffered heavy plane losses earlier, had to retreat, leaving the Marines without air cover. Nevertheless, the Marines held and improved their beachhead until they captured nearby Henderson Field. With their own airport, the Marines provided their own air cover, and six months later the Japanese were driven to evacuate Guadalcanal.

Fighting was fierce, and the United States nearly lost its carrier capability in the Pacific. The USS WASP was sunk. In October, the USS HORNER was lost. There was extensive damage to the USS ENTERPRISE and USS SARATOGA so that Admiral William Halsey had to appeal to Washington for help. In December 1942, Prime Minister Winston Churchill temporarily reassigned the British Carrier HMS VICTORIOUS for Halsey's use. It was assigned the temporary code name of USS ROBIN (for Robin Hood). So the war dragged on.

From the newspapers, we all knew James and Wil were training for some tough times if the war continued. Wil was very busy, and I'm sure James was also. Life at home went by at a fast clip. Wil was wondering in his letter of August 10th if we would have been better off had he waited to be drafted. But he said he guessed everything works out for the best, and he sure hoped so because we had gambled everything on his coming back and our being happy after the war was over. By mutual agreement, we did not talk of getting married and keeping it a secret any more.

On August 12th, he wrote, promising to come down the following weekend. He said they were flying two hours every day, trying to make the September 1st deadline. There was talk of bringing ten women to Clarksville to train as pilots. Wil hoped it would be after he left as he "Didn't trust women pilots any more than he trusted women drivers."

The next letter I received contained the snapshot they took of him the day he soloed. He was in civilian clothes, but, of course, he was receiving civilian pilot training (CPT) at Clarksville preparatory to going to Naval Flight School. A lot of boys were eliminated in CPT and sent on to another part of the service. It would have broken Wil's heart to flunk out.

On August 18th, Wil wrote that he and another boy were discussing the war and before they knew what was happening there were twelve or fourteen other boys in there arguing. Two boys got mad at each other and were not speaking. The school gave them a watermelon feast the night before, and they had a fight afterwards. He said that was the best part of it. Boys will be boys!

He did come to Pulaski the weekend before (the 15th and 16th) and we persuaded him to stay with us because James' room was unoccupied. He had come by bus and stopped to see his folks Sunday afternoon. He said his mother told him he would have to watch his Dad as he had fallen in love with me. That pleased me because I dearly loved his Dad and Mother.

Wil was prone to sudden spurts of temper, and I always

caught the brunt of it. I do not recall what he might have said that weekend, but in the August 18th letter he wrote:

> *"Darling, I'm sorry that I hurt you Sunday. You know that I can't ever love anyone but you. I guess I just wanted to be mean. I love you too much to ever change. You know that, don't you?"*

I did know it, and I loved him too much to not forgive.

18 WINGS & A NEW JOB

In the next letter Wil was worried because they were behind with flying, and the Navy would be unhappy if they did not finish in time. He felt they would start weeding them out and he might be one of them to go. But if so, he was going to try to get into the R.A.F. (Royal Air Force of Britain). Then he would have to go to Canada. I did a lot of praying those days. So, of course, that never happened.

On August 22nd, he got his cadet wings and rating. They had been rated Seamen Second Class but were now Cadets. That gave him about $21.00 more pay a month. He had to take his last flight check the next day with a Naval Inspector and was still concerned over being washed out. He wrote:

"At least you know what this means to me. Did I not give up the sweetest girl in the world for it? But I still love her more than anything else."

He passed with flying colors.

The last week of August 1942, they were really pushing the class at Austin Peay in order to finish by September 1st. They were training and flying about thirteen hours a day.

Meanwhile, I changed jobs. The General Shoe Factory offered me a job as Secretary. It paid $25.00 a week, versus

$18.00 at the bank. I needed the extra money, but the work was much harder. I was the only secretary with 500 employees. We shipped 10,000 pairs of boots to the Army at a time. Each pair had a long number and I had to list every number on the packing slips. This was done on a manual typewriter. I took shorthand from the manager and the district manager. I answered all the calls and took messages as needed. And I went up and down the stairs dozens of times each day. I started losing weight although I had none to lose. However, I felt I was doing something for our wonderful country.

About that time, Mama and Daddy moved to a new two story house on East Jefferson Street in Pulaski. We had a large yard, room for a garden, and a small barn for Mama to have a cow named Bessie. We had a chicken house with chickens and Daddy raised white rabbits to eat. Everything was rationed and a stamp was required for everything bought at the grocery stores, but with the garden, the cow, the chickens, and the rabbits, we had plenty to eat. My parents were always resourceful and also hard workers. And it paid off during the war years.

Wil passed his final flight check on August 25th and was classed as a Number 1 student by the Navy. I was so proud of him. We were both looking forward to the furlough he would have before going to Atlanta, Georgia.

James had been training at Paris Island and was about to be through. John Alton was about finished training and thought he might get to come home for the last weekend of August.

And September 3rd brought the news that Wil passed his final flight check by a government inspector that day. Only one boy in the class failed to pass, and he was given another chance. He said their instructor was happier than the pilots were because they all passed. The boys gave the instructors a party the next night. He said:

They looked like fathers whose wives were having a baby."

He heard from the Navy Department that they would be in Clarksville for eight more weeks of special training. So his furlough was postponed. Life was full of disappointments, and every part of life was dictated by the needs of our country and our "Boys". No one complained. We just did the best we could and prayed. There were only four boys chosen for the further training at Clarksville. Everyone thought they were lucky, but Wil was not sure about that because he did not really know why they were kept there. I was delighted because it delayed him from going overseas a little longer. Prayers are answered.

So September 1942 found Wil still in Clarksville. He was getting training in meteorology. He was still fretting over the fact that we had not gotten married. So when I wrote him that James Ed (Stooge) and Helen Holt had gotten married, I got a letter letting me know how he felt. He and Stooge were buddies, and we dated together some. Stooge worked at my Daddy's service station. Wil wrote:

"Well, I hardly know what to say about Stooge and Helen's marriage. Tell I sure had heart set on seeing the marriage performed. Tell them I wish them all the luck in the world. I kind of envy Stooge. I imagine it's kind of nice to have someone love you enough to marry you regardless. I think they used sense. Maybe they haven't got long together but even that's more than we had or probably ever will have. But we were going to be sensible. Maybe we were but look where it got us. Absolutely nowhere. But I suppose this is what you wanted so I guess you are satisfied but I certainly am not. Frankly, I live one life of hell. If something doesn't happen I am going to resign because I cannot go on trying to the work I have to do with only about half of my brain The other half is thinking of you and what might have been. It's that way all day long and I'm just not getting as much out of this as I should. I'm not blaming you because if you don't want to marry me you had a perfect right to refuse. But I guess when you want something as I want you, sometimes you overlook other people's rights. Oh, well, it's all in the past and it's too late to change things now so we will just

have to make the best of it."

Dear Reader, if you remember anything about me and Wil Cordell, you must know how miserable it made me when I felt I was not pleasing him. He really wanted his cake and to eat it too. To be married and still be a Naval Cadet. We both knew that was not possible.

19 SEPTEMBER & OCTOBER 1942

After that letter, I wrote that I would marry him regardless. He came down the weekend of September 19th, and we made plans to get married the following weekend. Thomas and Sarah were planning to get married that weekend. Wil would come here with them, we would go to Athens, Alabama, where we could get married without a waiting period. It was three days waiting in Tennessee. We would tell everyone we were just going to be with Thomas and Sarah, but no one was to know we were to be married also. I walked on eggshells all week, excited and frightened of what we were planning.

A letter from Wil on September 22nd was full of apprehension also:

"I have done so much thinking since Sunday that I'm about nuts. But after all that I am no nearer a decision than I was Sunday. I know I seem crazy even hesitating a minute after I have asked you so much but there is so much in our way. I love you so much that I don't even want to think of anything else but still there is one thing I can't forget. If I was certain it could be kept a secret then everything would be ok but......."

He went on to explain that if I told my mother we would have to tell his, and the more people who knew, the more danger the Navy would find out. He would rather just resign than get a dishonorable discharge. He was going to try to get to Nashville early enough on Friday to see a Naval Officer he knew and get his advice. But he would definitely come with Thomas and Sarah and if I decided definitely that I wanted to get married, we would do it regardless. So the ball was back in my corner.

I remember being a nervous wreck all week. The thought of doing something so serious without telling my Mother was unthinkable. But I was determined to do it if Wil still wanted to.

Friday night found me dressed in my best and ready to go when Thomas, Sarah and Wil picked me up. It was later than we should have been, but I guess the marriage license office stayed open late on Friday nights to accommodate those coming from neighboring states. Wil and I were sort of subdued and quiet on the way down. But Thomas and Sarah were very excited and happy. We finally arrived at the courthouse. Wil and Thomas went in while Sarah and I waited in the car. Wil looked so good as he was wearing a khaki uniform by that time with a matching khaki cap with a bill.

They came back to the car and got in saying we had to go somewhere else to a Justice of Peace. I knew something was wrong with Wil. I asked, "Honey, did you do it?" He said, "No, I changed our minds." It was both a relief and a disappointment and one of the best decisions we ever made. I assured him I was all right with it, but he was not too happy. We got Thomas and Sarah married and started back to Pulaski. It was Thomas' car and he was driving. On the way back, I remember asking Wil how he felt and he answered, "Like a damn fool." They left me in Pulaski and headed back to Nashville. They would have had to do that even if we had tied the knot because Wil had to be back in Clarksville Saturday morning. We both knew we had done the sensible thing once more. They got back to Nashville at 2:30 AM so Wil did not get much sleep. I'm sure I didn't either.   I told my parents the next morning what had gone on, and they were happy we waited.

But Wil still had not given up. He wrote me on Sunday from Clarksville that he might have a solution for us. He would not tell me what it was until he could talk to the Navy officer friend in Nashville. I don't think he ever told me what that plan was.

He had tried to extract a promise from me that I would come to Nashville the following weekend if he could come home. I don't know what I said but I must have made him mad because he wrote:

"Mary, I got mad Friday night and I am sorry but after I have been down there as much as I have and then you say what you did I couldn't help but get a little mad. I told you this would probably be the last weekend I could go home. I think it will be but if you don't want to come that's ok. I will be home for furlough November 1st. I think I will finish my flying before then . So if you don't want to or can't come I won't get mad about it. But I am not coming down there till you do come. Write and tell me as I don't think I'll go home unless you are coming. I love you very much and miss you more. Love Always."

For some reason I could not go to Nashville that weekend. But he did not fuss about it so I guess I had a good reason. He wrote that he would get two or three weeks at home when he finished in Clarksville. And he hoped we could figure out a way to get married during that time.

"I sure hope we can. If we don't, I guess we will just have to go on hoping. If we should I don't know whether I can stand it or not. I'll be so happy to get away from here and then getting married too may be bad for my heart. But you are bad for it anyway."

The next letter I have was written October 13th 1942. He was telling me about an Army plane that cracked up the last week about eight miles from Clarksville. He went to see it, and it sure was a mess. One boy was thrown about 100 feet and his brains were lying on the ground. I really needed to hear that. I lived in fear of something like that happening to Wil.

He was able to come to Pulaski the weekend of October 17th and 18th. From his letter of the 20th, it must not have been one of our better times together. I imagine we were unable to agree about getting married because he wrote:

"Mary, I don't know what was wrong with us this weekend. Every other time it is my fault that we argue but this time you seemed that way. And I was really serious about getting married this weekend but you didn't seem very interested so I got tired of mentioning it. I guess it was a lot my fault but I love you so much that I guess I'll always love you no matter what".

He was really tired of Clarksville but had only about two more weeks there. I guess I wrote what was needed to get back into his good graces because he wrote me on October 22nd and said he stayed at school while the other boys went to a dance so that he could write to me. He said it had rained so much they would not get their flying in but he was ahead of the rest of them. He thought he would be through by November 3rd, and the others would have to stay until November 15th. He had offered to come to Pulaski and work at the station so my Daddy could get some much needed rest. He wanted me to find out what Daddy had decided . Daddy had lost a lot of weight and was working too hard. The election had been a disappointment so we were all hoping he would take advantage of Wil's offer. And of course, Wil and I wanted the time together.

He wrote:

"Mary, did you know that I love you very much? If I didn't, I could go to the dances and date other girls and have as much fun as the other boys. But I had rather have you than all of their fun. Even on the weekends that we fuss so much I enjoy being with you more than anyone else."

How could I help loving that man?

20 NOVEMBER 1942

According to a letter he wrote October 27th, I was planning to be in Nashville the following Saturday, and he was coming home. He was wishing I could come on Friday because Elizabeth Ann (Pansy) was having a party. But I could not get off from work early enough because we were so busy at the factory.

However we both made it to Nashville for a Saturday night and Sunday together. I am sure the entire Cordell family was there except for John Alton. That was October 31st and September 1st. One of my young sisters was with me. We rode the bus to Pulaski on Sunday night, and a white man and a black man were arguing and about ready to fight. So Daddy said I could not ride the bus anymore because of the racial friction. He very seldom said what I could or couldn't do, but he was worried about my traveling around with only one of my sisters. I was hoping Wil could come here to Pulaski for part or most of his furlough.

It was really hard to be so much in love and never really have any time to be together alone. We were constantly in company of one or other of our families. But that was the way it was back then, and families were close. We accepted it as the way it was and were thankful for any time where could see each other no matter how many were there. My parents would never have let me travel anywhere to see Wil except to Nashville when he would be at home.

Finally he saved a letter from me and I still have it in the company of over 700 others letters we wrote each other during the war. He had been so sweet over the weekend in Nashville that I wrote and told him I loved him much better when he was sweet. I also told him that one reason I was afraid to marry him was his tendency to be hateful at times. I was afraid he did not love me when he was hateful to me. He wrote back that he wished he could pound it into my head that he loved me more than anything no matter how he acted. He was becoming a tough Marine and I was always rather sensitive to any harshness. He was never ugly or mean to me, just treated me like he owned me. And I guess that was the way I wanted him to feel.

Wil finally had his flying and his exams behind him and was back in Nashville for the long awaited furlough. He was home on November 2nd. He said he had really been taking it easy, sleeping late every morning. He was planning to come to Pulaski but wanted me to tell him when. He wrote:

"Honey, I guess this will be the last time we will be together for a long time, so if you want to get married while I'm down there just say so. This is our last chance so what we do this time will be final for a long time, maybe always. Think it over and let me know as soon as possible. What I want Is not the question - it is what you want. You say I never do what you want me to, so here's one time I am."

I guess I would never have gotten over it if anything had happened to him and we had never gotten married. But the same
reasons were still there for waiting , so I opted out again.

At this time, James had been transferred to Jacksonville, Florida where he was training as a Marine navigator. He hated Jacksonville but we were happy and thankful that he was still in the States and getting more training.

I wrote to Wil to try to come to Pulaski by November 10th because Paula, my sister, was going to be in two stunts at Stunt Night at the high school. In my letter to him of

November 7th, I had been trying to work out a way to give him what he wanted. I told him we would just get married and tell no one. But I stressed over and over in the letter that we would have to be careful and he would have to know what to do to keep something from happening that we would have to tell. I certainly would not know what to do. I can't believe now how innocent and naïve I was, wanting to marry someone so badly but not able to bring up the subject of "I might have a baby". How times have changed!

Donald came home that weekend for several days so Wil would not commit just when he could come down. He wrote that Donald broke a date with Hilda the night before so he and Wil could see each other. So she was mad at Donald. But Wil said I wouldn't believe how good he and Donald were, and they got home early. Donald spent the night with the Cordells. I wound up sort of upset myself because Wil did not come down when I wanted him to but he and Donald had been friends for so long and Donald was on his last leave before being sent overseas. So I understood how Wil must have felt. Wil wrote as soon as he got his visit in with us, he would have to report for duty also. He said:

"I'll be ready to go. You are the only one that I really miss an awful lot and I miss you while I am here so that won't make much difference. I love you very much and wish I could have you with me always but that is just one of those things. "

Wasn't he sweet? I thought so.

He did not come for Stunt Night but I went without him. My letter that day was short and cool. I felt he would have come if Donald had not been home. I did write that Whitfield McCracken and Bill Maultsby were at home. They were headed for the Pacific, and James would be also if he had not qualified for further training. Prayers were still being answered.

Bill came over to tell us goodbye. That was the last time we ever saw him. He was killed on Bougainville Island.

Before I mailed my "cool" letter, I wrote another one at work apologizing if I had sounded hateful, but I was just so disappointed when he didn't come.

But he did come, we did not get married, but we had some time together. He worked with Daddy while I was at work. He stayed at our house and we probably went to a "picture show" every time the program changed. At that time, Pulaski had two movie theatres, THE BEST and the SAM DAVIS. Strange that now 70 years later they have none.

That was a wonderful two weeks that Wil was here in Pulaski. He just became one of the family. James was able to get home at that time and several of Wil's family came for a day. Aunt Louise, Uncle Gilbert and their daughter, Corinne, were here also. So it was like a family reunion with only a part of the families. We had a photographer come and take our picture as a group.

And then, all of a sudden, it seemed, Wil was in Athens, Georgia as a Naval Cadet. He may as well have been in Africa because it seemed so far away to me and travel was so restricted. The first letter I have from him was dated November 23rd and he was to leave for Athens on Wednesday, the 25th. I am going to copy the letter because it is such a sweet letter, and I want to share it with anyone who is interested in just how it was to be in love with a war going on and never know what could happen from one day to another. But you have to remember, I felt guilty and ashamed when I let him kiss me. I was raised so strictly to be modest and always a lady.

It turned out that I did get to Nashville in time to see him off. I got off early on Wednesday, November 25th and rode the train. I got there in time to have a few hours with him and his family. We all went to the train station to see him off. I wrote him a letter later and told him that I may have seen him off without coming apart but if he didn't believe I cried when the train pulled out, he could just ask his older sister, Evelyn. I think I went off to pieces. I stayed that night and the next day with the Cordells. Then I went home to begin my wait for him to come back.

Letter from Wil to Mary, written November 23, 1942,
after spending two weeks in Pulaski with the Whitlock family.

"My Darling:
I guess it seems kind of silly to write to you tonight but I
miss you so much that I thought maybe writing to you would
help but I doubt if it will.
Mary, its all over now. We have planned on getting
married so much that it seems that is all I can think of but I
don't want to think of anything else. I wish we had gone
ahead and planned to get married Tuesday night even if we
would not have had but one night together. Even that would
beat what we have now. But if you think it is better this way
then this is how I want it. Thomas and Sarah have just left
and we went to the show. I don't know how many times I
started to say something to Sarah thinking it was you.
Seeing them together sure didn't make ime feel any better
either. They certainly seem to be really happy. But I guess
you are thinking that I made my choice between you and the
Service and took the Service so therefore I deserve to feel
like I do. I guess you are right about that too but I will say
that if I had loved as much in June as I do now or rather in
the same way I do now, I would never have joined. But I
guess I wouldn't have been satisfied with other boys leaving.
Darling, I have never felt so blue as I feel tonight. Other
times when we have planned to get married and didn't I said
to myself, "Well, we still have other chances. " But now I
know that we have made the final decision that will have to
be final for a long time. But until it is changed I'll keep o
loving you remembering these last two weeks. Nothing can
ever destroy or take them from us. At least we shall have
that much.
And, Darling, I am sorry for what I said that hurt you and
for how I acted. I am not sorry because I think less of you
but because you said you would be ashamed of it. I am
sorry that you are ashamed but I don't suppose you would
believe me if I told you that it made me think more of you.

That's the truth even if it is not right.

Dad and Mom were talking tonight about us getting married. They both said if it wasn't for the Navy, nothing would please them any more than for us to get married. And I really think they meant it. They both said some mighty swell things about you. Dad said you were far too good for me and Mom said that I had all the boys beat on girls, even Thomas. So you see they really want us to marry if that is what we want. I'm afraid if they had given any more encouragement, I would have come back down there tonight and married you. But I was afraid as I have been all along that you didn't want it as bad as I do and would only do it because I wanted it so badly. But if ever in these next 8 or 10 months the Navy changes their rules, you can consider yourself as good as married whether you want it or not.

I can only hope that you want it half as bad as I do. But, Honey, if you should change your mind, please let me know. It would end just about everything for me but I'd rather have that than have you unhappy. I guess you think I should have felt like that when I joined the Navy but as I said before I love in a different way now.

Darling, I'm afraid I won't get to see you again before I leave. I may have to leave earlier Wednesday than I expected but I will call you tomorrow to tell you and see whether you can get off or not.

We got a letter from John Alton today. They have been put on the alert and that means that they are getting ready to sail. Mom has been crying nearly all day. Dad looks worse than she does. So, Darling, even if you can't come in time to see me off I want you to come anyway and maybe that will make them feel a little better. I hate to ask you to do it but I know how this place will be Thursday.

I am going to the country tomorrow and see all of the folks. They would never forgive me if I didn't. Mom and Auntie are going with me. I hate to see Auntie when I leave about as bad as I do Mother.

Well, Darling, I guess all of this sounds silly but I feel a little better now. So remember that somewhere always there is a boy who loves you very, very much and will miss you

*even more. But you will always be close to me to help me. I
am counting on you. So until……*
   Love Forever,
   Wil

NOTE: I hope everyone understands that I did love Wil
enough to marry him and I never understood why he always
seemed to blame me for us not doing so. I think he just
wanted me to insist so he could be sure that I did love him
as he loved me. I loved him enough to be willing to wait for
him to get his beloved Wings as I would never have forgiven
myself if he had been discharged for getting married and had
to fight on the ground, which he would have hated. And as I
have said before, we never did anything with each other to
be ashamed of or embarrassed over.

21 ATHENS, GEORGIA

Except for working eight to ten hours a day at the Shoe Factory, I spent my time making embroidered pillowcases, hemming cup towels and hoarding back anything I could afford to put away toward the time I would be a housewife, although that seemed to so far in the future that it all seemed a futile endeavor. I wrote to him every day as soon as I received an address.

The first letter from him was written November 26th. He had just arrived in Athens, Georgia. They were going to be training at the University of Georgia campus. He wrote that he felt it was going to be really hard there. He confirmed that he loved me very much and he did not know what he would give to see me. His address was:

Cadet W. E. Cordell V5
Room 121 Langley Barracks
Navy Pre-Flight School
Athens, Georgia

A short letter written on the 27th told me he had his physical that morning and he thought he passed. Of course, he did. He was a perfect specimen of manhood. (Was I prejudiced or what?)

He always told me he loved me in every letter.

So a new kind of life began. America was a busy nation, most single women were working in all sorts of jobs usually held by men. The shoe factory was going full blast getting Army boots ready for the troops. Pulaski was booming as we had several factories that were switched over to make war supplies and gear.

The depression had been forgotten. Everything had been rationed but no one complained as it was for the boys and the war effort.

On November 28th, 1942, a bad thing happened in Boston, Massachusetts. A fire touched off by a busboy's match, swept through the artificial palm tree decorations in Boston's Coconut Grove Nightclub. The subsequent holocaust killed 491 people, including many servicemen celebrating before being shipped overseas. America grieved.

I spent that Thanksgiving with the Cordells in Nashville and rode the bus home later that day. I guess Daddy had lifted the bus-riding restriction. In a letter I had ready to mail as soon as I received his address, I wrote that Evelyn, Denny, Pansy, Mother Cordell and I went o Lawrence and Myrtle's for he day. I told him I brought his brown suit home with me, and Mother Cordell had given me the money to have it cleaned and put in a mothproof bag. So I had something of his to keep. I wrote of plans to start buying some furniture as soon as I got a studio couch I had bought paid for. I told him I wanted to show both sides of the family that we were trying to be smart and do something toward the future. From the first, I seemed to be obsessed with working and saving our money. I did tell him I wanted to be out of debt before we started saving because we'd never feel like it was ours as long as we owed someone else. I was wondering if it would have been easier to be separated if we were married . I closed telling him:

"Write often and never forget that wherever you are there is a girl waiting for you to come back".

Seventy three years later, I still feel the pain and anxiety of our being separated but now I know that he is not coming back.

On November 29th, I wrote that I had packed James' Christmas box so we could mail it by December 1st. We knew that neither he nor Wil would be here for Christmas. That was the day I got a letter from him with his new address, so we were back in touch.

Wil wrote me on November 29th. He had been to a movie on the Post that afternoon. It was THE GENERAL DIED AT DAWN. He said it was *"pretty good"*. He wanted to hear from me, but he knew it would be another day or two anyway. They had to go to Chapel on the Post on Sundays. He sent me a printed program of the service, but the print is too dim to copy now. It was quite an impressive affair. The Cadet Choir sang several songs. The Chaplain's name was Lt. M. H. Twitchell, Chc.USN. There was some audience response as well as audience singing and lots of pomp and ceremony. I think Wil really enjoyed being in that atmosphere of worship. What we were both raised in and were used to was so much more simple.

In that letter of the 29th, he was telling me how much he missed me. He wrote:

"I didn't think I could ever love anyone as much as I love you. I'm not even letting myself think of all of this time we will be apart, only of the time when we'll be back together again and nothing can ever separate us again. I can't say when that will be but I only know it can't be too soon to suit me. I don't care what happens, I will always love you and will always miss you when I am away. I sure hope you feel the same way. If at any time you don't, please tell me. You know what I told you about keeping me satisfied. That still goes and I hope you don't let me down. I love you too much to ever be away from you one minute but this is something we cannot help.

Be good, Honey, and keep loving me."

The requirement for keeping him satisfied was to write every day and not even look at another boy. It was easy to keep both of those conditions. My whole life was wrapped up in my Wil.

He started a letter to me on Monday the 30th and finished it Tuesday night. He still had not heard from me or his folks, so he was feeling left out. But I mailed a letter the minute I got the address. Mail was slow as everyone was trying to stay in touch with the fighting men. Our whole world rotated around those who were gone.

He wrote that there were 1850 boys in the training program at Athens. I'm sure they were not all in Flight School. They had two nights of lectures on "Naval Traditions" so most of them must have been training as officers. They were treated very nicely, played jazz music thirty minutes before their supper each night. Wil and I liked Sammy Kaye better than any other band. Glenn Miller was good also. Other favorites were Guy Lombardo, the Ink Spots, and don't forget the Andrews Sisters.

I wrote to him on November 30th also. My little sisters were all at a birthday party and Daddy was working at the station until l0 or 11 p.m. most nights. So Mama and I were alone. She was dozing, so I was telling how lonely I felt. I wrote:

" *I'm just like the song - I'm not sick, I'm not blue, I'm just plain lonesome for you."*

I was encouraging him to study hard and make good but I told him:

"If you do much more than you've already done, I might get the big head. You know I'm awfully proud of you."

November 30th was the night Evelyn had all the Cordells who were at home for a birthday party for Mother Cordell (Nur). I wanted to go but couldn't get off again so soon. I told him that Nur and maybe Gram and I were planning to come to Athens to see him Christmas. But if we didn't get to, I would spend the Saturday and Sunday after Christmas at his folks. We had all drawn names for Christmas giving and I had gotten Myrtle's name. (She was married to Wil's oldest brother, Lawrence). I told him the radio was playing "When the Roses Bloom Again" and it was so pretty.

22 EARLY DECEMBER 1942

I had more trouble putting my feelings on paper than Wil did. But I did write in that letter:

"Well darling, guess I'd better close. There are so many things I could say but it might sound rather foolish in writing. You know that all the things I do not write are there just the same. Cause I think you know how much I love you even if I haven't the words to tell you. But sometimes I wonder if you'll ever really know how much I love you. I know you'll never know how much I miss you. But you will be home before long and I am just living for the day.
So Goodnight, Sweetheart, and never forget......
Your Mary."

My Mother always had so much company it was hard to find a quiet place to write my letters. On December 1st, I wrote that we had thirteen people for supper and they were all in the room where I was trying to write. I told him with all that crowd I was still lonely. Uncle Gilbert and Aunt Louise always came to our house between jobs. He was a foreman for a construction company. They built highways all over the country. So they were at home with us at this time. Before she married, their daughter, Corinne, was with them. Her little dog, Prissy, came with them also. Corinne became more like a big sister than a cousin.

I was still making plans to try to see Wil at Christmas, but travel was so hard then that I was afraid I would not get to go. I still have the Christmas card my family sent Wil that year. Of course I sent him a box of gifts later.

He had gotten my first letters by the time he wrote December 2nd. He said he was sorry I cried the night he left Nashville but was glad I cared enough about him to cry. He wrote:

"I wish I could tell you how much I love you, but it would take a lot more time than I have to tell you all that. I wish it were so we wouldn't miss each other because I know I could do a lot better if I didn't think of you so much.

I can't say I miss you more than I did before I left, because I missed you too much before and I haven't fully realized that we won't see each other for three months."

In that same letter he wrote that he was the Mate of the Deck for the day and was not supposed to be writing letters. He loved to live dangerously. He did not like being Mate of the Deck because that involved just sitting and monitoring what was happening on the floor. He said the pace they kept was very hard but the officers were nice, given their commission to teach just one thing. Their wrestling instructor was an Inter-National Champion as were their swimming instructors. He said he shared a room with three other cadets. One was from Texas, one from Oklahoma, one from Washington, D. C. and of course, he was from Tennessee. He said the barracks were nice, almost new. There was 50,000 acres on the Post, and he claimed they hiked over all of it the day before. He was not allowed to tell me some of the things they were studying, but he would tell me anyway if he thought I would understand it, but he knew I wouldn't. He did soften that in closing by saying:

"Goodbye, darling, and remember I love you lot more than I should not being married to you. Love forever."

Mary W. Cordell

Letters were our lifeline to sanity. We used to have
colder winters than we do now. I wrote Wil on December 3,
1942, that it had sleeted all day and everything was a solid
sheet of ice. We were expecting snow before morning. I was
still hoping to work it out so I could go to see him the
Christmas weekend. My boss said I could be off on
Thursday (the 23rd)if I needed to but the trip seemed such a
big undertaking to me. I had never traveled much and
certainly not alone. The trains and buses were so crowded,
and the government begged everyone to stay at home
unless it was a necessity to travel. I wrote that I had a letter
from Pansy, we had two from James and that Aunt Louise
and Uncle Gilbert were still living with us. Daddy had sold
900 gallons of gas at the station on Monday but only sold 12
gallons on the day I was writing - Thursday.

We had a two story house, heated only with coal burning
fireplaces. I don't know how we kept warm, but we
functioned very well. Mother had a small coal burning stove
that heated our water. That was kept going all the time
because we used it for baths, washing clothes and cleaning
purposes.

I wrote him on the 5th that the snow and ice had thawed
a little the day before but had frozen again during the night.
It was sleeting again. I had made it to see the "picture show"
DESPERATE JOURNEY, the night before. I'm sure it was a
war picture. I told him I would not try to come to Georgia for
Christmas. I could only be off for Christmas Eve and Day.
Instead, Nancye and I would go to Nashville Christmas Day
(Saturday) and spend the night. I always closed telling him
how much I loved and missed him.

I started another letter that same night and finished it on
Sunday. I had escaped to the library Sunday afternoon and
was enjoying the peace and quiet. Our household was
always a happy, busy place, and almost always we had
company. I told Wil that I had checked out a book called
AVIATION CADET written by a boy who got his Wings at
Pensacola, Florida. I wrote:

"I think I will read everything I can on airplanes. I am

trying my best to learn to love them like you do so maybe it will help if I learn to know them better.

Being in the library is so quiet that it makes me think of some of the times when we were together and I would quit talking. Then everything was so quiet because you never said anything much, did you? But you said enough to make me love you forever. Don't ever forget that, darling."

Wil wrote on December 6th that he had a letter from me that day, Sunday, and he was the only boy who got mail that day. He said he sure rubbed it in on them and told me not to let him down by not writing. He got a fruitcake from his mother and candy from Evelyn and Clifford's wife, Elizabeth. He said he didn't get to keep much of the candy but still had one-half of the cake. He was dreading Christmas because he said all they would do on the day was stand up in class and be silent for fifteen seconds. He said one boys said "Hell, when I was home I used to start celebrating two weeks ahead of time and took three weeks after Christmas to get over it." Wil said the most important rule they had there was: "No drinking of beer, wine or whiskey shall be permitted." He said they kicked our more boys for that and cheating than anything else.

The following is a letter, verbatim, from Wil to Mary from Athens, Georgia written December 5, 1942. What a year it had been.!

Dearest Mary:

Well, I have already written several letters tonight and I have about written out, but since you come first with me I just have to write to you too. I have been getting your letters every day. I got the one you wrote Wednesday night this morning. It sure makes me feel better too.

After the first two or three weeks, I think I'll like it a lot better but this last week has been the most miserable I've ever spent. I wasn't suffering physically but mentally. I think I could be perfectly satisfied if I didn't love you so much. I didn't know how much I did love you until I came down there and stayed. I don't miss the folks at all. But I don't think I'll ever get so I won't miss you.

We had exams this afternoon. In some ways it was really simple but some parts of it were hard. I think I have found out what I'll do when I get my commission (if I do). They have been complaining about not enough boys volunteering for fighter pilots. They say they are afraid and a lot of stuff like that. I don't know what's wrong but most of the boys asked for instructor jobs. There were just a few of us who asked for fighter positions. I sure hope I get it. They asked us to list our choices and we had five choices so I put fighter pilot first and instructor last. I don't know how much it means but I hope it goes through.

Well, Darling, I've about written out. I could write several More pages on how much I love you but I think you know..Always remember that I do now and always will. Write often and leave those soldiers alone.

Love as Ever,
Your Wil.

23 FIRST ANNIVERSARY OF PEARL HARBOR

December 7, 1942 - one year since Japan attacked our fleet at Pearl Harbor. I was having a quiet night at home. Mama, Daddy, Nancye, Uncle Gilbert and Aunt Louise had gone to Uncle Buster and Aunt Frances' house for supper. I could not get off early enough to go so Paula and Peggy stayed at home with me. We walked to see a "picture show" with Humphrey Bogart in ACROSS THE PACIFIC. We walked both ways and got home about 10 PM even in the cold.

In my letter written to Wil that night, I wrote:

"You said you loved me too much not to be married to me. I think I love you more than most married people I know love each other. But maybe I can live through it knowing how happy we will be when you come home."

That same day Wil wrote that it was raining so and was so cold that it was more like snow in Georgia. So they had been in their rooms all afternoon. He said he and his roommate had been fighting the Civil War for hours. They called a peace treaty to write letters. He said he had his roommate reading the Bible (the seventh chapter of I Corinthians). In that letter he was back on the subject of getting married. He wrote:

"Darling, I miss you so much. Sometimes I wish I didn't love you so much, but I'm sure I could not love you much more than I do now. I can hardly wait until March. I haven't decided whether we shall get married then or not. But I am pretty sure we will (that is if you want to. Do you?) I hope you do. Sometimes I wonder why you love me at all, but I guess it's impossible for anyone to be loved as much as I love you without at least liking them In return. Know that I love you and will never change. Yours forever, Wilburn".

The postman was so good to me. When he would see I had a letter from Wil, he would deliver it to the factory so I would have it sooner. He would even bring us letters on Sunday from Jimmy and Wil. We all felt each other's pain and anxiety.

My letter of December 8th told Wil that I had really been blue all day. I had walked home even though it was already dark, but I said I was glad to walk because it made me feel better to walk with the wind blowing hard in my face. Kind of clears your brain, I said. I told him I started to just keep walking.

Wil had written that they were having exams. The highest grade you could make was 4.0, and at 2.5 you had failed. He had made 4.0 on the two exams he had heard from. He had also written that he had signed up for Fighter Pilot, and I was telling him how proud I was of his grades. But it was always hard for me to be encouraging about his being a pilot because I was so afraid of it. But I did tell if that was what he wanted to be (a fighter pilot) that was what I wanted him to be.

On December 8th, Daddy, Uncle Gilbert and Uncle Rowe (Mama's brothers) went hunting and killed 49 squirrels. We had 34 of them, so I told Wil we would be eating squirrels until Christmas. Meat was rationed, so people depended on hunting and fishing. Mama had her chickens and Daddy his rabbits so we had meat. I signed off that night telling Wil we had been listening to Bob Hope on the radio and Skinny Ellis was singing "Every Night About

This Time". Who was Skinny Ellis???????

On Wednesday night, December 9th, I stayed home from Prayer Meeting. Peggy, nine, and Nancye, five, stayed with me. I wrote they were playing Santa Claus with Peggy as Santa and Nancye as a little girl waiting for him. My sisters were a great pleasure to me. I was their second mama, rolling up their hair every night, making some of their clothes, buying things for them. I have never really outgrown the feeling of being responsible for them. I wrote Wil:

"You said you had been hoping I didn't miss you as much as you missed me. Well, I've been hoping the same thing. It is bad enough to be away from home much less to feel like part of yourself is in one place and one part carrying on your usual work. And that's the way I feel. Someone will say something to me and half the time I don't even hear them. My mind just isn't on anything here. I still feel like it would have been better if we had married. We would have had so much more . You know being away from each other is just like death. Of course, not really as bad. But what I mean is you want to do something about it so bad and yet all the time you know how little you can do. So we will just have to wait, darling, whether we want to or not."

Now, after all these years, I realize how true those words were then and now. With death- there is nothing you can do but wait.

Training in Athens proved to be pretty rugged. On December 9th they had to hike 15 miles. They started before daylight and carried five station wagons to bring back the injured and those who could not take it. Three boys broke their legs, and Wil did not know how many passed out. The legs were broken jumping off a bluff across a creek. Wil carried one of them a mile. Then when they got back from the hike, they had to go to athletic for exercise. This was on a Wednesday. Another hike was scheduled for Saturday. He did not get a letter from me that day, so he was feeling neglected as well as tired. But he wrote that he wanted me to come Christmas if I could although he would not have much time off. He closed with:

"I love you very much and wish this was my wife I was writing to instead of my sweetheart but I love you just as much."

Dear Reader, if you get tired of all our lovemaking by letter, remember the book is about a "Love so Dear".

24 CHRISTMAS PREPARATIONS

December 10th at our house was an evening that seldom happened. It was quiet and peaceful. Uncle Gilbert and Aunt Louise were spending the night with her folks. Paula and Peggy were spending the night with Aunt Jim. Mama and Daddy went to a "picture show". I was alone with just the cat and the dog and Nancye asleep with "Henry Aldridge" on the radio. What a treat! I wrote to Wil:

"You said you did not know why I loved you. I get to wondering how how you ever put up with me. But I just love you and can't help it. I"ll admit there have been times when I wished I did not love you but not lately I feel like if anything should ever happen I didn't have the right to love you I would just go crazy. I am leaving March up to you. I made up my mind what I want while you were here and I think you know that it is "Yes".

December 11th was a lovely day, weather-wise, and I was worrying that Christmas would be nothing that year with Wil and Jimmy both gone. Jimmy had gotten his box from us but was saving it for Christmas. He sent $20.00 for presents for all of us, but we decided to put it in his savings account. $20.00 was a lot of money in 1942. Jimmy sent all he could home to be saved.

It seems I was never satisfied. The little sisters were across the street playing when I wrote December 12th, and I was wishing they would come home because I was lonesome. Mama and I were alone. Daddy worked late on Saturday nights. Mama and I had gone Christmas shopping that day. I got Mama a chenille bedspread, and together we got Daddy a robe and bedroom slippers. Nancye (5) had gone for her Christmas shopping that morning. I told Wil, after seeing what she bought, I started to let her do my shopping. I also told him:

"But I declare if she keeps on she'll be hanged before she is ten years old. But she sure is cute if she is mean."

She could hardly wait to go with me to Nashville for Christmas.

At about that time, Uncle Gilbert had all of their furniture brought to our house. Don't ask me how we ever made room for it, but we did by storing some of our things.

I finally told Wil that I would not try to make the trip to Georgia. We would not have any time together with his tight schedule but, oh, how I wished for the times when I would be looking for him to come on Saturday night or early Sunday.

On Sunday, December 13 the last of Jimmy's buddies came to tell us goodbye. He was Merlin McCormack, and the draft finally got him. I told Wil I cried when he left. Jimmy thought so much of all the boys he ran around with. Merlin had been in my class at school. He volunteered for the Ordnance Corps of the Army. He made it back from the War but died a few years later from some strange disease.

I was wishing I could see Wil in his uniform and was begging for a picture, so he sent me some snapshots. I received a pretty long letter from him, written on Sunday, December 13th. He had gotten a letter from me on Sunday again. He said he liked that because that was when he missed me the most. He was remembering one year ago (December 14, 1941) when Thomas, Betty, Wil and I had planned to go to Pulaski and something happened that we did not. But he wrote:

"I guess that was one of our first disappointments. If we had only known then how many more were to follow. I sometimes wonder if it was meant for us to be together. But if I didn't believe that we would be together someday I don't know what I would do. I guess it is a good test of love. If we can stand this, I think we can stand anything. It probably wouldn't be so bad if we were married. Then we would know for sure that we had something to build on. I guess we have more than some people do anyway. I had rather have you like this as to having any other girls with me all of the time. A day with you is worth more to me than a lifetime with anyone else."

A letter like that meant more than all the world to me.

At that time, things were changing for them. All dress parades were done away with, and he said they hardly ever wore their dress uniforms anymore. He was addressing his Christmas cards and wishing I were there to do it for him. He said he tried to call both his Mother and me on the 12th but could not get the calls through. We had none of the sophisticated methods for keeping in touch that we have now. The postal service was overworked. We used telegrams for emergency communications, but words were limited.

The Post in Athens had a nice indoor swimming pool, and Wil used it every chance he had. He wrote on Monday night, December 14. The whole country was busy, and everyone was focused on winning the war. He said his Mother wanted to know what he wanted for Christmas. He wrote:

"I didn't tell her because I don't know myself. I don't even know of anything I need except a certain very sweet little girl, in fact, the very sweetest. Since I can't have her I don't care for anything else."

He was telling me to listen to the radio the next thursday night because one of the Coca-Cola Light Bands would be entertaining them, and it would be broadcast over the radio. The band was Jack Teagarden's.

The next several letters were ones I wrote to him, and they were never as interesting as his were to me. I was suffering with a cold but kept working. Aunt Frances' mother was very sick so Mama went there a lot to help out. On December l5th, it was unnaturally warm, but we were going to put up our Christmas tree that night. I went a week without hearing from Wil, so I was getting worried. We were not hearing as much from Jimmy either, but we knew they were both busy. Jimmy was still in Jacksonville, Florida. I still have the Christmas card my folks sent to Wil and one he sent to them in 1942.

Finally I got a long letter from Wil written December 17th. He said they stopped them from writing letters during study hours. They told them to write them on their own time, but he said they had no time on their own. He claimed they only had 25 minutes of their own time, and they had to make up their beds, wash, take showers, shave and clean up their room in that time. Wow!

John Alton was getting ready to sail. I got a Christmas card from him but did not have an address as to where he would depart from. All of Wil's school chums were gone except Frank Bradley and Ben Hill. William Pulley and his brother joined the Army. Donald Robinson had sent his personal belongings to his Dad, so he was ready to sail. Petie Edwards was in the Service but would get home for Christmas, and he and Nancy O'Reilly were going to get married. She planned to go back with him. He said:

"Maybe it won't be many more months before we can get married. At least I hope so. I'm getting so damned tired of something keeping us from getting married, I don't know what to do. I make out very well down here until I get to thinking about us and then I can hardly stand this place. I don't suppose I am as bad off as some of the boys because they do treat us decent. We are supposed to be officers now and conduct ourselves as such. I never got so tired of hearing one thing in my life as I have that. We cannot

smoke on the streets, even in town, because it is not becoming to an officer. Everything we do we have that preached to us."

Of course, I had written him also on the l7th. I wrote every day but that day I had finally heard from him. I was telling how much I had to do besides working. I have to get packages mailed, get ready for the church group I was entertaining the next Monday night, get all my "Santa Claus" for the girls together and finishing decorating the tree. On top of all that I had just mopped the kitchen. I was also reminiscing over everything that had happened to us since December, 1941 and how different things were. But in spite of everything I was happier in 1942 because we loved each other. I wanted so badly to go to Athens to see him, but they were begging us over the radio to stay at home. I just hoped I could get up to his folks on the 25th.

25 A CHRISTMAS APART 1942

On the 19th , I wrote that Uncle Gilbert's furniture had arrived, and we all had to work so hard to get it polished up and the house rearranged to fit some of it in. I was mailing his and Jimmy's Christmas boxes that day. I'm sure those boxes were Christmas goodies since we waited so late to mail them.

My letter on Sunday (20th) found me sad and lonesome. It was raining and supposed to snow. It was real cold,. After church I had listened to Sammy Kaye. That always made me long to see Wil. The War songs were so beautiful. I was telling him how sore I was from all the furniture lifting the day before. I thought I had strained my back. I only weighed 100 lbs., but I could do my part of hard work. I was wishing again in that letter that we had gotten married and that I was coming to Athens to see him for Christmas. But everyone was in the same boat and some of the husbands and boyfriends were in combat on both sides of the world. Some were never coming home. At least Jimmy and Wil were still in the States

The letter he wrote me on the 20th said that he had been able to loaf most of the afternoon after church. They had to attend the services on the Post. He said he had gone to see a show (on the Post) called NOW VOYAGER, but he had already seen it when he was visiting us in November. He wrote:

"What I wouldn't give to be there right now. I don't ever once think about wanting to go home. All I think about is coming to you. If it weren't for you I would not even be here. That is kind of hard for you to believe, isn't it? It is too much to try to explain now but if you will remind me of it when I come home, I'll tell you all about it."

I do not recall his ever telling me what he meant, but I think he felt he would have left Clarksville sooner and joined the RAF so he could be flying and already in the War. He was impatient to be in the thick of things and only stayed with all the training because of me.

He said he got so hungry for real Tennessee cooking that he would even eat a meal that I cooked. He would never brag on my cooking to me but would tell others how good my cooking was. He would say, "If I eat it, you know I like it." He did write that he was just living for the day I would cook all of his meals. He hoped that would not be too far in the future. He was complaining about the monotony of what they were doing and how slowly time passed. He wrote:

"They say the purpose of this school is if you get killed in War, it will make Hell seem like a vacation. I am almost beginning to believe it."

But everyone was wishing for time to pass and the War to be over. But it was only just beginning.

He had wired my Mother some roses for Christmas. She got them and was very excited. No one had ever sent her roses before.

He was wishing us all a Merry Christmas because he thought this would be his last letter before Christmas.

My letter written on Monday (21st) was going on about how I missed him as much in the morning as I did at night. I had to go to work, and that night was when we were having a bunch of the young folks from church to eat and then we were going to go out caroling Christmas songs on Thursday night. So we had to practice. I wrote the next morning that I had fifteen guests to practice singing, and it went well. I was hoping I would never spend another Christmas without him. I was granted that wish, and we were together every year after 1942. Our last one spent together was 2003.

My letter of December 22nd told him I had gotten a set of linen guest towels from my friend in Gallatin, Frances Hollins, and a box of candy from a soldier, John Neely. He was stationed in the Hawaiian Islands and had ordered the candy from a company in New York. I had known him through my work with the USO.

The other news in that letter was that Jimmy had sent a $50.00 money order home to put in savings. He was richer than any of us! I had finally gotten the rest of Wil's Christmas gifts and would mail the package the next day. They were pictures and were just not ready in time to get them to him before Christmas. I told him after seeing them I did not think they were ready yet. Other news was that I was playing with Jimmy Hosay's baby that night, and she was so cute. Cecil Brock had passed his physical and would have to leave next Sunday. Poor Mary! She was only sixteen. I told him they were taking a bunch of married men.

He did get to write to me on the 22nd. He had the watch duty at the Main Operation Building and was not nearly as busy as he thought he would be so he wrote to me. He had gotten my big package. I had sent a lot of baked goodies, and I don't remember what else. I had given him a fountain pen before he left. He said they were going to get liberty of Christmas Day after all. Had I known that I would have gone to Athens. He wrote:

"I sure wish you were coming because I'd give anything to see you I was talking to a boy in the room next to mine today and he said he wrote his girl and asked her if she wanted him to come back and marry her. He told me if she said yes he was going to do it and the Navy could go straight to H____. Sometimes I feel like coming back and marrying you, if you still want me. You know this Christmas was the first date we set to get married. We had no idea that there

*could be anything to stop us. I sure wish there wasn't. If I
have to go on much longer like this, I will go nuts. I thought I
wanted the Air Force more than any- a thing else in the
world, and I guess I did until I spent those two weeks down
there. Now the Air Corps is a poor second. I don't suppose
you could guess who or what comes first? Maybe
something will happen and I can have both, but I doubt my
having such luck."*

Nancye and I went to Nashville Christmas Day. My visit
with the Cordells was always so wonderful. We all went to
Charlotte Dunn's wedding and then Pansy, Nancye and I
went to a show downtown. We saw HENRY ALDRICH FOR
PRESIDENT.

That was on Christmas Day. Evelyn (Wil's sister) gave
all the sisters-in-law (Becky Frost and me also) some
dresser sets she had crocheted. Pansy gave me a
paperweight with the White House in a globe. When you
shook it, the "snow" fell.

What on earth became of it?

26 CHRISTMAS LETTERS

Lawrence had drawn my name, and he gave me a nice leather chest full of stationery. It had little drawers in it. Mother Cordell gave me a sweet baby picture for my room. I told Wil that his family was well. Evelyn and Allen had gone to see his folks, and I still had to see Clifford and family. Pansy had gotten a puzzle for Christmas, and we were having trouble doing anything with it. Wil was really good at puzzles. I wrote:

"Well, we just got your letters. It was awfully sweet of you to write to me up here. I'm glad you wrote your Mother too. Darling, don't think I didn't remember that this was the first date we set to get married. And I'm not forgetting either that one year ago tonight was the night I realized I was in love with you. But please do not quit the Air Corps on my account. Maybe the Navy will change its rules or maybe we can hold out till you get your Wings or maybe we can get married and keep it from the Navy. There are things beyond just getting married and we have to think of the future. I wish I was there when you are on Guard so I could sit there and talk to you. I think we are going over to Auntie and Uncle Horace's for supper tonight. We miss you, Darling.

Wil called that night and talked to all of us. That was a

real treat. The next day, Nancye and I came home. We did not have to travel by bus. My boss, Mr. Bowers, and his wife were coming to Nashville on Christmas Day, and they brought us up and then took us back home. It was pouring rain. In fact it was raining everywhere because Wil's letter of the 27th said they had gotten do much rain and were behind in getting to fly so he thought he would be there eight to twelve more weeks. They had gotten their uniforms. He liked the blue ones but did not like the white uniforms. He had a lot of trouble writing that letter because of breaking his thumb and a finger boxing. But he thought my pictures were pretty and *"could he have a date with me when he got home?"*

He sent me six $2.00 bills to save for our honeymoon.

Pansy had come home with me, so we were going to a show most every night. I really loved having her there. Uncle Gilbert and Aunt Louise were leaving on December 29th to go to a new construction site. Letters from Jimmy were so blue at that time. He wanted us to try to come to Jacksonville when he graduated because he felt they would be sent right on overseas. We were having such a hot day on December 28th that I was afraid we would have a storm. I said it was so cloudy and hot that it felt like Summer. I was planning again to try to come to see him.

I wrote only a short letter on December 29th because I was writing it at midnight. Pansy and I had been to a church party at the Coca Cola plant. I told Wil there was such a crowd and that Pansy made a hit with Logan Fox. She was so pretty, she was a hit with lots of boys. Joyce invited Pansy to come to her house the next day. I had to work. Joyce and I were on speaking terms again. She had a new boyfriend and wound up getting married before Wil and I did.

She had seven children, so Wil sure lost out there. I told Wil I got the six $2.00 bills and put $5.00 with it and the bills were in our cedar chest.

On December 29th, Wil wrote that it was still raining so hard they let them stay in their rooms for almost two hours. He and his roommate (who was married) started arguing over whose girl (or wife) loved them the most and they were still arguing that point. His hand was a lot better. He wrote that in three more weeks, they would be the Senior Battalion. They would get lots more privileges such as being able to put my picture out where it could be seen. He was wondering how many more weeks it would be until we could see each other. That was his last letter in 1942.

I wrote on the 30th that Pansy, Mama and I had gone to Prayer Meeting and it was 10 o'clock. Daddy had gone to a rationing meeting and was still not back. Pansy had spent the afternoon with Joyce, and Joyce came back to our house with her to go to church with us. We all walked everywhere we went. I was really missing him. I was wondering how much longer I could stand it. I told him just knowing he cared made me feel lots better. I said:

"I wonder if there has ever been another girl whose boy was as good to her as you are to me. I think we have a standing date for life."

My last letter for 1942 was on December 31st. My family was alone in the house for the first time since he came down in early November. Uncle Gilbert and Aunt Louise were gone. Pansy went home that day. We all decided to go to the picture show and see Jack Benny in GEORGE WASHINGTON SLEPT HERE. We were too lonely to stay at home. I had another cold, and the nurse at work had put me on vitamins as well. I had too many colds. That letter was short. I did not feel like writing. But we wound up the year still madly in love, still wishing to be married, still planning on a long life together, and wondering what 1943 would bring.

This is the letter I wrote on Christmas Eve, 1942. I still have the locket he sent. Must have used up the compact.

Christmas Eve, 1942

Dearest Wil:

Well, here it is Christmas Eve at exactly 10:30. Paula and I are here by ourselves as we have just come in from carol singing and wound up at the Mansfield's house and had eats. I have had a pretty nice day. I got off at 1 o'clock and took the kids to the show, then shopped around a little. I am really tired tonight though.

Darling, I can never tell you how proud I am of the compact and locket. They are just beautiful but even if it had been a handkerchief I would have been prouder of it than anything else I got. I just feel like you shouldn't have gotten me so much though. But words can never tell you how much I appreciate them. Mom got the roses last night and she was tickled pink. She said tell you she certainly thanked you. I got a box of candy from Mr. Bowers (my boss) today and the Chief Inspector sent me a Christmas card with $2.00 in it for doing his typing. Mom and them are giving me a small cedar chest for my letters and such as that. Everyone here is having a pretty big Christmas. Of course, we had rather have you and Jimmy home as everything money can buy.

This time tomorrow night I will be with your folks. They are my folks too. Mr. Bowers and his family are going to Nashville tomorrow so Nancye and I are going with them. I miss you here, Wil, but I will miss you much more there. I know because I have never been there without you, and too in Nashville nearly every place I see I remember something we did there, something that you said to me and things like that that makes you feel worse when you remember them.

You may skip a day getting a letter. I hope not, but I know you will forgive me if you do. I have gotten a little mixed up in the way I mail my letters so you'll get one every day but I have just been so busy. I will try to get straightened out again as soon as I get back from your house.

One year ago tonight or rather today, I got my watch. I saw Joyce today and I couldn't help but think how different this year is from last. Wil, I love you so much more this year than I did last. I simply begrudge every minute away from you. You said you could almost eat some of my cooking now. As soon as we get over the Christmas rush I will cook you something and send it to you. And believe me, I am ready to cook all of your meals the minute things are so I can.

I'm as bad (almost) over the gifts I got from you today as I was over the ring. I just had to show them to everyone. The postman brought them to the factory so everybody down there had to see them.

Paula and I have already put all of my gifts under the tree. I don't know how Mom & them think Santa Claus will come tonight if they don't come on so the kids can get to bed.

Well, Darling, speaking of bed I'm sleepy. I miss you so much "Every Night About This Time". And I love you and thank you again for the gifts and for being so sweet to me and to Mom.

Your Mary

This is the letter Wil wrote to Mary on Christmas Day, 1942 from Athens, Georgia.

My Dearest Darling:

Well, this is another Christmas Day almost gone and we didn't see each other. I don't know why but I've kept hoping all day that you would change your mind and come down here. I knew it was hopeless but I couldn't help wishing.

If I could have spent this day with you then everything would be OK. But its just one of those things that we just seem to be having plenty of, even more than our share.

This has been a pretty long day for me. We got up at 7:30 and had to go to Chapel. We got back from there at 10:30. I don't think we ate any breakfast because we were saving for the dinner. It was good. The Chaplain gave us all a New Testament for Christmas. He made a pretty good talk. *We got liberty this afternoon till 6 o'clock. I put on one of my roommate's enlisted uniforms. Those blue ones.*

You should have seen me. The reason I wore it is because they get more privileges than we do because most of them are married and their wives are here. My roommate and I went into town last night and ate supper at one of the big hotels. I really enjoyed it.

This afternoon we went to the train depot and watched the train come in. I would have given my right arm to have been getting on it to come home. Not home but you know what I mean.

I haven't heard from you since I got the cake Tuesday.

I don't know why but I haven't. The mail came in today but I didn't get any mail. I hope you have been getting my mail OK. I haven't been able to write as much as I want to but I have written as often as I can. I hope you got your Christmas present OK. Thanks for mine. and believe it or not I'm actually using the cigarette case.

Well, they are having a show for us tonight and its about time for formation so I guess I'd better close. Please excuse my writing but I broke my thumb boxing yesterday I think maybe another finger is broken but I'm not sure. They are going to make an x-ray of it tomorrow. Well, so long, darling, and be good. Hope you had a good time up home.

Love, Wilburn

Mary W. Cordell

27 JANUARY 1943

Apparently January 1943 came in with beautiful weather. I wrote Wil that it was so pretty I was tempted to go outside and play. Instead I cleaned out my cedar chest on January 2nd.had a letter from Jimmy with some pictures of him in uniform. I meant to have copies made to send to Wil, but my Mother accidentally grabbed them up with other papers and burned them, If you wanted to save anything on paper, you had to hide it from my Mother. She could not stand clutter. I must have kept my letters in my cedar chest, or we would not be reading them today.

I wrote on Sunday, January 3rd, that I was so lonesome. I wrote:

"Darling, I wish I could see you. Just to say Hello if nothing else. Sometime I wonder why I don't go ahead and go crazy from missing you instead of fooling around about it. I wonder if you will ever know how much I depend on you. You are really all I live for. I try to do so much for my sisters, thinking maybe that will keep me from thinking of you too much but they don't interest me anymore like they should."

Wil wrote me on January 3rd and said they were having pretty weather also. He wrote:

"The stars are sure pretty down here. We have a lot of

114

pine trees around here and the moon shines through them just like you see in pictures. If I had you here I could really enjoy it."

He told me he loved me more every day.

By the time I wrote January 4th, it had really turned cold again. I told him I had to walk home from work and the wind nearly froze me. I told him I cut through the graveyard so if I disappeared they would know one of the "boogers" got me.

Even with gas rationing, people still bought all they were allowed. I told Wil that Daddy sold 250 gallons of gas on Saturday and again on Monday.

We heard from Jimmy and he had averaged fifth highest in his class in their last study phase. And he was the only one in their class of 100 who could keep up in a blinker quiz test. That was something about radio. As usual, I was complaining of being lonesome for him. I told him so many girls I knew were getting married that we would have to have a big church wedding because we were going to be the only couple left who were not married.

On the fifth of January, there was a turnover of management at the Shoe Factory, so a new man came in. We had been listening to "Fibber McGee and Molly" on the radio. Unless we went to a picture show, radio was all we had for entertainment.

In January, 1943 a new kind of mold, discovered on a cantaloupe in an Illinois market yielded nearly ten times more penicillin as previous sources. It was quickly placed into mass production to alleviate the critical shortage of the antibiotic. It was a big boon for the wounded soldiers.

My letter to Wil on January 7th had the news that my cousin, Roberta, who had a job in Nashville was coming down to see about a job that was open at the Shoe Factory here. I felt sure she would get the job, and I was excited over her working with me because we were always big buddies. She did get the job.

Wil wrote on the 8th that it looked like they would finish up at the University of Georgia by February 16th, and he was supposed to have eight days before having to report to the new base for more training. He wanted to be sent to Memphis, but it was full at that time, and he doubted he would get to go there. That began the anticipation of a few days at home.

My letter of January 7th (the second for that day) is sort of puzzling as I told him I had just written him a long letter but tore it up because it was silly and too much on one subject. I told him I was asking him to forget all about everything I had ever said or done that was unwise.

"...the least bit unwise. I think you know what I mean. We can start all over when you come home and maybe my conscious will let me alone."

I have no idea what I was talking about except I think I always felt guilty that I loved him the way I did. I know I worried that God might punish me for putting Wil on such a pedestal. I know for certain that I never behaved in an "unladylike" way, but I did permit a lot of "petting". Oh well, God did not punish me. He let me keep Wil for 61 more years.

I cannot believe now when we talk in terms of millions and billions of dollars, just how much a dollar meant back then. Wil had sent the six $2.00 bills earlier, and I had put $5.00 with them so we now had a total of $26.00. (I guess I had added another dollar.) I wrote that wasn't a bad start, and I would put it in the bank until we had enough to buy a bedroom suite.

Jimmy was winding up his studies in Jacksonville and wanted us to save our gas so we could come for his graduation. He knew he would be going overseas with no furlough. But I knew I could not get off from work, so I would not see him before he left. But this was wartime: everyone was sacrificing.

The War was raging on both sides of the world. In January, MacArthur's "leapfrog" strategy went into effect. The strategy, jointly credited to the General, and to Admiral Theodore Wlkinson, called for the bypass of strongly fortified enemy bases, moving around them to establish new U. S.

Bases closer to the Japanese homeland. The enemy bases were then to be sealed off from fresh supplies by U. S. air and sea power until they capitulated. I guess that proved to be a good strategy.

A letter from Wil written on January 10th in answer to my silly letter of the 7th said:

"It seems a little hard for me to understand. I have a general idea of what you are talking about but outside of that I'm left in the dark. Maybe it's because you have changed your mind or something, but this seems kind of sudden. I didn't want to forget and I didn't think you did either. But I suppose you have changed. Do you remember what you said the night I left you? You said that you were glad of everything because that was about all we had left to remember. I can't tell you how great that made me feel. I know it is hard to keep feeling the way you did when you are afraid that I might change. If I could write to you more often, then that might help keep you assured that I won't change, but, darling, I write as often as I can. I know if I didn't hear from you any more than you do from me, it would make me a lot more doubtful. Maybe we can get married in March."

He was so sweet and understanding at times, and I guess my problem was insecurity. I felt that he could not possibly love me as I loved him. Love makes you crazy sometimes.

I wrote him immediately to disregard the letter I wrote. I told him I used to think we might change toward each other but after the two weeks he spent with my family and me in November, I had no doubts about either of us. I told him I thought it took those two weeks for us to both to know where we stood.

Oh, how I wish it were possible to relive those two happy weeks with my parents and my little sisters and Wil there with us just as if he had always been a part of us. Even if Jimmy was not there, we knew he was alive and all right in Jacksonville. And now here I am, with Peggy and Nancye in Texas and everyone else gone.

28 WINTER DOLDRUMS

January dragged on with the usual gloomy days interspersed with some Spring-like days. I had started packing my lunch to cut down on walking back and forth in the cold. The factory would shut down for the lunch hour and was so quiet after the noise of the machinery overhead. I looked forward to Roberta coming so we could eat lunch together. Her brother, Jimmy Phillips, had also gotten a job at the factory so that worked out well for them.

We had a big jukebox in the office. Most jukeboxes took a nickel to play, but this one played by just pushing a button so we would play it at lunch, and some of the factory girls would come in and dance.

I had a letter from Wil (January 14th) telling me that he had heard from Frank Bradley, a Nashville buddy. His news was that he would go into the Army in March and Ben Hill was going in May. Also Petie Edwards and Nancy O'Reilly got married at Christmas as planned. So many of Wil's old gang waited to be drafted. Thomas Hamlett was still out, so he and Sarah were having some time together. It was strange in Pulaski with so many of our boys gone.

On Saturday, January 16th, Mama and Nancye rode the train to Elkmont, Alabama to visit with her brother, Ben, and his family. Paula and I were at home alone; Peggy had gone to the show with a friend, and Daddy was still at work. I had gone to the dentist that day and was being pitiful because my gums were so sore from cleaning and two fillings and I had to go back the next Saturday for more fillings. But believe it or not, I still have most of my teeth.

Wil was back on the subject of getting married on the furlough. Each of us wanted the other to make the decision, but we all had the same reasons for waiting. On the 17th, he wrote:

"Mary, I know I have asked you to marry me lots of times but for the last two or three weeks I have been thinking about it more than usual. I think if we hadn't joked about it so much we would be married right now. But that is all past, there is a future, you know, even if it is just eight days. I think the future has stood in our way too long. The reason I am telling you all this, is this is really our last chance until I get my commission, at least because the last time I will get to come home."

He thought he would be home between January 25th and March 1st for eight days but he couldn't know for sure when.

The Service was very strict regarding the conduct of officers. One of the boys Wil trained with in Clarksville got into trouble. When he was home in November, he spent several nights with a woman whose husband was in the Army Air Corps. The husband came home, found a letter the boy had written the wife, and wrote to their Commanding Officer. The boy was subject to Court Martial and a dishonorable discharge for conduct "unbecoming an officer". Wil said he had heard that phrase until he was sick of it. He told the boy to try to resign and avoid the dishonorable discharge. Wil was slipping around to write to me because they were allowed only certain times for personal use. Of course, I worried he would get caught and be in trouble but I did cherish his letters.

I wrote on the 20th that Roberta was here and spent the night before with me.. We had gone to the show and saw ME AND MY GAL. I thought it was the best show I had ever seen, but now I can't remember a thing about it.

Our new boss, Mr. Buntley, had a new baby, so the company nurse stayed with his wife for three or four days. I was drafted into wrapping cuts and treating burns suffered by the employees. I like to do that, but I never was a very good nurse.

The Gas Rationing Board told Daddy he could not use his station gas to go to Jacksonville. So we were all blue over maybe none of us seeing Jimmy before he went overseas.

Elizabeth Ann (Pansy) and I were keeping in touch by letters, so I knew the Cordells were all right. Like me, they lived for letters from the "boys". I was really missing Wil and I wrote:

"It makes you just feel like you could fight, scream or anything else just to have things back like they were and our boys at home again".

The nurse was still gone and I was juggling two jobs and getting very tired.

A letter from Wil on the 22nd was telling me that time was passing more quickly than it did earlier because they were so busy. The sport of the week was football, and he liked it so much better than any other sport, so he guessed that was why time passed quicker. He said they sure played rough, but they were tough Marines by then. Several boys got hurt, but the doctors just ran out on the field and picked them up and the game went on. He said three doctors followed them around when they had sports and also on the rifle field. He said the doctors got plenty of business, but so far he had not gotten hurt.

They were going to make them wear their new blue uniforms the next day, but he wasn't too happy. He wrote they were giving them a party the next night and bringing in 800 girls from Atlanta. There were only 700 servicemen there. He said he was not going to the party because it seemed silly to him. I never asked if he went or not. He was thinking if he could just be sent to Memphis we could get married on his leave.

They did not get to fly in Georgia because of more officers training and learning all the things they had to know to function as war pilots. I knew he was getting anxious to get back into a plane.

On January 24th, Wil called. I guess the call helped both of us. He wrote me a long letter that night. He was reminding me that January 25, 1942 was the night he brought a friend from business school and me to Pulaski, and he went to see Joyce to tell her they were through. He wrote that if we didn't get married before he got his Wings, there would be little reason to marry because he would be going overseas. He said:

"If we don't marry while I am home, I am going to quit planning on it because I feel that if we think chances are too much against us now, then the chances will surely be greater then, because I'll be gone a long time probably and the chances of ever coming back are too slim. I know you think I am crazy for feeling this way but I just can't help it."

I had no intention of letting him go overseas without putting a ring on my finger and his. He said he still did not know when they would be finished there – that they expected an officer to be able to run a ship as well as an airplane. When he finally would get his commission, he would have seventeen months in the Navy. The Army Air Corps required eight or nine, so most of them were sorry they did not choose the Army. He finished that letter with:

"But regardless of everything else, I love you very much, darling, and I guess I always will. It would take lots more than us not getting married to make me stop loving you."

That was a red letter day for me.

Photo left:
MaryCecil Whitlock
1941

Photo right:
Mary
1941
"The outfit I had on the
first time Wilburn saw
me."

**Photo left:
Wilburn & Mary
1942**

**Photo right:
Wilburn E. Cordell
1942**

Top: Photos exchanged while Wilburn was training in Clarksville, TN. Both were nineteen years old.

Bottom right: Mary, 1943.

Bottom left:
July 30, 1942. Taken after Wilburn's first solo flight, Clarksville.

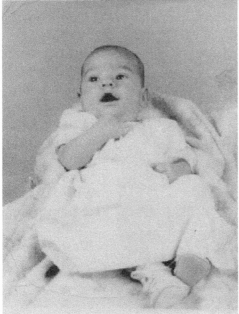

**Lt. Wilburn E. Cordell &
Mary W. Cordell, two days
after their wedding, August
30, 1943**

**Our precious son, Gerald
Dykes Cordell, three
months old.**

Photo top left: Lt. Wilburn E. Cordell, January 1945. Just prior to being sent to the Pacific.
Photo top right: Mary Whitlock Cordell, 1945. Twenty-two years old. Sent to Wil while he was serving on Iwo Jima Island.

Photo bottom left: Lt. Wilburn E. Cordell, U.S. Marine Air Force, taken while serving in the Pacific during World War II. This photo is in World War II Remembrance Building in Washington, D.C.

29 TROUBLE IN PARADISE

I wrote to him after the call also. I told him I was so lonesome after hearing his voice that Mama and Daddy felt sorry for me and me took for a ride and to see the Buntley's baby. I also explained why I hung up so fast on the phone – I didn't want him to hang up first.

Apparently we were having very cold weather in Tennessee the last part of January 1943. Everything was solid ice on the 26th when I wrote. But I guess we were getting to work some way because Roberta was going to spend that night with me on account of the weather.

I was hoping we could get married on his leave that was coming up. I didn't know how I could wait until he got his Wings. And I was really hopeful he would be stationed in Memphis.

Then there was trouble in Paradise!!!!!

Remember the elderly postman always brought my mail to the factory, so I could have it early? He was my friend. He brought me a letter on the 26th, and I was so happy to get a letter two days straight. Then he handed me a second letter and asked if I would deliver it also. When I looked at it, my world came apart. I will never forget how I felt at that moment. The letter was addressed to Joyce, but he accidentally used my address. Oh, Wil, how could you write to her when I had been subject to snickers and giggles behind my back by Joyce and her friends? I changed the address and gave it back to Mr. Ethridge. I know now I over reacted but at the time my trust was destroyed. I knew Mr. Ethridge had given me the letter on purpose because everyone who knew us knew the situation. I'm sure he thought I should know Wil was writing to Joyce. I had asked Wil not to write to her. I finished my day at work, but my mind was in turmoil. I felt so betrayed. I could not wait to get home to let him know how I felt.

I really wrote a strong letter on the night of January 26th, and I'm sure when he got it he felt really bad. I could understand why Joyce was trying to get back close through Pansy. And I had tried so hard to be nice to Joyce because I was afraid we had hurt her. It turned out she was already planning to marry someone else, and her writing a pitiful letter to Wil was just an attempt to break us up and then throw her new love in our faces. She almost succeeded.

Wil had written me again on the 26th, but, of course, he was unaware of my turmoil as yet. He was all upset because they had been told that day they would be in Georgia five more weeks, so he really had the blues. He had a fight the night before, and he thought they were going to kick both of them out and especially him because he refused to apologize to the other boy. But his swimming coach told him not to worry about it because he would see it did not even go on his record. I never learned what the fight was about. He spent a page of the letter telling me how much he loved me and missed me. Mother Cordell (Nur) was sick at that time so he was worried about that.

Good intentions and all that, I could not stand not writing to him. So I wrote again on the 26th. I told him I did not mean to write until after I heard from him about Joyce, but I had decided that if we let things like that come between us, we might lose each other, especially while we were so far apart. I admitted I was silly to jump to conclusions about his writing Joyce, but it hurt to lose faith in someone you love. I told him if he wasn't ready to give Joyce up completely, just not to mention getting married any more. If he was ready, then I wanted to get married when he came home. I had mailed him a package for his birthday. I can't recall what I sent. I will copy the letters pertaining to that episode just to show how true love just cannot let go.

I made up my mind that nothing was going to stop me. I was going to Georgia to see Wil, and I wrote him on January 29th that I was coming. That was before I received his letter of the 29th. I had asked off from work and had checked on bus schedules and I was going the first weekend in February unless he wrote and told me he wouldn't be able to be free to see me. I sent the letter Special Delivery, and he got it that Sunday. He immediately wrote the letter dated January 31. It was really hard for Wil to have to explain his feelings to anyone and harder still to apologize. But I always told everyone there was a side of him that only I knew, so I want everyone to see how he really was to me. You will see that in the copy of the letter he wrote on the last day of January, 1943.

January ended with me planning to go to see him. The episode about the letter to Joyce was one thing in my life I kept to myself. That was out of character for me. But no one knew how upset I was. I learned from Evelyn that the family thought I was going and that we planned to get married. So I guess they knew I was upset over something. Evelyn said my Mother said she didn't think we would marry that weekend but she was sure we would if he got any time off in March. But Mama told Evelyn she was not going to say anything if we did because she felt they had all interfered enough

Amidst all of this, I had a letter from Wil's good friend, William Pulley. He had been drafted into the Army three months before. He said he had been in Kentucky, Georgia, Alabama, Louisiana, Mississippi and Texas but he still loved Tennessee better. He was being shipped overseas but he did make it back from the War.

Letter from Mary to Wilburn   January 26, 1943

Mary W. Cordell

Dear Wilburn:

I hardly know just what to say or how to say it because I don't know just exactly how I feel. The postman brought my letter today and I was so happy over getting a letter two days straight and then he handed me another letter and asked me if I would deliver it for him as he was not coming on this street. Naturally I took the letter and I don't believe that I would have felt any worse if he had hit me because it was to Joyce from you. You had, I guess through mistake, sent her letter to my address. I was so shocked I couldn't talk but I finally made him understand where she lived. Wil, you said that I could keep you satisfied in Georgia. I agreed to try to. I haven't dated, I've tried hard as everything to keep my part of the bargain. I haven't complained when you couldn't write so often. But all the time, Wil, I thought I could trust you. Now I understand why Joyce and the crowd she runs around with seem so cocksure. I heard Joyce talking about you in Kuhn's the other night. I simply said to myself that I shouldn't worry because I knew that you wouldn't write to Joyce behind my back. I even told Mother so. And I haven't told her about this afternoon either. Maybe it would help some if I could just cry and get it off my chest. Wil, of course, is your privilege to write to whoever you please but what hurt me so bad was that you should do the only thing that I asked you not to do and do it behind my back. I guess I see now why Joyce could come to my own home and make her brags about how she knew you would come back, that she knew you better than anyone else in the world. I just let that go by, too, because I told myself that no one knew you better than I because no one could ever love you as much as I do. I told you, Wil, that I wouldn't write if I found out that you were writing to Joyce. It just seems unfair to me that you should expect me to do every bit of the giving and you not do that one thing for me. It is not that I think you are writing to Joyce in the wrong way. It is just that you don't understand and haven't tried to, how much I have to take from that crowd of girls anyway. Imagine what I feel like being around them when they know that you are still writing to the girl you used to go with. Regardless of what you write about no one ever reads the letters but Joyce.

I am not even mad, Wil, I'm just hurt worse than you have ever hurt me. After getting your letter and that piece, Wil, I think I could have made up my mind. In fact, my mind has been made up since Thanksgiving but you have a decision to make yourself, Wil, and this time it has to be made once and for all. You tell me you care nothing for Joyce and you expect me to believe it while you are still writing to her without my knowing it. I love you, Wil. If I didn't, would I care? Waiting to hear from you.

Mary

P.S. Please forgive me for writing anything that might make you dissatisfied but you seem to forget that it's just as hard to sit at home and wait as it is to be away. And I have to know, I just have to know for sure one way or the other. There's only one thing more I want to say – I thought I wanted to know if you were writing to Joyce but I would give the world tonight if the postman had never handed me that letter. When I saw it I felt like my whole world had opened up and swallowed me. I'm not asking you not to write to her. I simply want to know what you are going to do. You don't ever have time to write to your own Mother and she has been sick but is better now. Nothing serious, Pansy said, but I know she would like to hear from you. I love you.

Letter from Wil to Mary   January 29, 1943

Dearest Mary:

Well, I guess we are more or less in the same position. I don't know what to say either. I had hoped that I wouldn't have to write it but could tell you in person. But two things have made that impossible. One thing, your seeing the letter to the other and the other is I won't get to see you for about 9 months. They have cancelled our leave that we were *supposed to get when we finish here. But, of course, that is beside the point and doesn't even seem important now. I know you want to know what it is all about. I wish you had opened that letter and read it, then it would have been much easier for me to explain. But since you didn't I guess it's left up to me.*

Well, first, you are right in thinking that I wasn't writing to Joyce because I loved her. I think you know that I don't love her. I know it's hard to believe now but it's true.

Now, as for what Joyce and her friends think, that should be the least of your worry. If it isn't, then just for me, every time you are around any of them let them know that I said I would marry you any time I could and please emphasize that it is my idea for you know it is. If you do this I don't think it should leave any doubt in any one's mind who I am in love with.

Mary, I meant to tell you all about this as soon as I came home, mostly because I really wanted you to know so it wouldn't seem like I did it to your back. Of course, its too late for that, but if you do believe what I say, then believe me when I say I made a choice last year, of which I am very glad and I don't want to change it. I love you lots more than you think. I would give anything if I hadn't hurt you, but I thought if I could tell you myself, it wouldn't hurt you. If you had gotten mad then I wouldn't feel so badly about it. But it just shows again how much better you are than I. I have told you before that you were too good for me but you wouldn't believe it. At least, this proves my point.

Darling, I haven't changed my mind about marrying you. I really intended to marry when I came home but, of course, that's out. But if you still want to please say so and it will make me feel better. Either way couldn't make me feel much worse.

I still haven't told you why I wrote to Joyce. I won't try to tell you in this letter but if you want to know just say so and I'll write the whole thing. I was answering a question she asked me. I wouldn't care in the least for you reading it. I hope this makes you feel better. If this is not enough to convince you of how I feel, then let me know and I'll start all

over again. Well, I guess I'd better close.
Yours Always,
Wilburn

Letter from Wil to Mary   January 31, 1943

Dearest Mary:

I had just started writing to you when the messenger came in and told me to come to the office. I couldn't imagine what it was. It was the letter you wrote Friday night,. The one this morning was the best letter I'd ever gotten but I think the one I got tonight was still better. Darling, you know I want you to come especially since I won't get to see you for a long time.

I guess you had not gotten my last letter. I have been in hopes that they would cancel the order that took away our leave but I don't think they will.   It was so sudden that I could hardly believe it at first. Until I got your letter today, I assure you that how long I stayed here was the least of my worries.   I guess you know what was worrying me most. If you don't then I won't try to tell you. Mary if you were to quit me I don't know what I'd do. Since last Spring, it has never seemed possible that I could ever love anyone as much. I still feel the same way, only more so, If you had the least idea what you mean to me then I don't think you would ever worry about Joyce or anyone else. I thought I loved Joyce once, but if that was love I hate to describe what I feel for you. Maybe it's because we have had better encouragement from both sides of the family than most couples have. We have been lucky in that way but it seems like luck's against us in every other way.

Mary, you said I deserved the letter that you wrote. Darling, I think that letter did me more good than any you have ever written. If you had told me you were mad and not particularly hurt, it probably wouldn't have meant much to me. When you said that I had hurt you worse than I ever had, you don't know how deep that cut. You know when I was trying to tell Joyce that I was through that was what held me back. I did not want to hurt her. Well if you have the least idea of how much I love you then you know how I felt when I got your letter. When I wrote that letter somehow it never occurred to that it would hurt you. So Darling, I think if you can forgive me I, then I think maybe I can love you a little more. I can't promise because it seems impossible to love anyone even half as much.

Darling, you sad if I didn't intend to give Joyce, up not to mention getting married again. I have given her up long ago but I won't mention getting married anymore. I will leave it up to you.

Honey, I got the bracelet yesterday. It sure is nice. I don't know how to thank you enough. I was very careful to notice the postmark on your letter and the package. It sure made me feel better that the package was mailed after the letter.

Well, Darling, it's almost time for taps so I'd better close. I'll get the room at the hotel for you. I can be with you from 2 till 6 Saturday afternoon, 7 till 10 Saturday night and maybe all day Sunday. I will be looking for you Saturday.

Love Always,
Wilburn

P.S. I want you to take the money I sent you to come down here on. You had better not be here unless you do.

I called home today. Everyone is OK. Mom is sitting up. I talked to Evelyn, Denny, Elizabeth Ann and Mom. I tried to get you but the line from Nashville to Pulaski was busy. I would have given anything then to talk to you but after getting your letter, I feel OK now.

30 FEBRUARY 1943

I went to Georgia the next weekend. Pansy could not get away to go, but the two families were not willing to let me travel alone, so Evelyn came down on an early bus that Friday. She and I left Pulaski at 1:30 pm and arrived in Athens, Georgia at 9:30 am Saturday. We had a three hour layover in Chattanooga and again in Atlanta. Wil had a room reserved at a hotel in Athens. It cost $4.00 for us to stay one night. The weekend went well. We all three had a good time and Evelyn saw to it we had some private time. We left him about 8:30 pm Sunday night and got to Pulaski about noon on Monday. I came back reassured that "My Love So Dear" was still mine forever, and I felt that I could make out without seeing Wil until he got his Wings.

Coming home from Georgia, we had some excitement on the bus. The bus was already packed, and the driver stopped and took on some black people from the side of the road. There was a member of the Legislature on the bus and he got so angry. He and another man got off in the middle of the night with no sign of anywhere they could go. He got off saying he would bring up a bill in the Legislature about it. He did not accomplish a thing except to make everyone mad at him and wasted an hour of our travel time. But we still got home in time for me to work half a day on Monday. Evelyn spent the night and went home Tuesday.

Apparently, Wil gave me some money he had saved because I wrote him I would take our money to the bank the next day. I wrote:

"Well. Sug, it will probably be a long old time before we have any more weekends but I am going to try to make up my mind to waiting until it can be otherwise. I'm trusting in you, Wil, to make my waiting worthwhile. And I know you will not let me down. I really believe that. And you know I will never let you down.

P.S. Nancye (5 years old) just got back from the show and some little boy had kissed her. She told Daddy, "Some little boy kissed me and I just can't get over it" She doesn't know the half of it"

I wrote Wednesday, February 10th, that I was listening to someone on the
radio singing:

"Weep no more, my lady, weep no more,
Stand behind the guy that you adore,
And when you see him walk in your front door,
Then you'll weep no more, my lady, weep no more"

I do not recall the song now, but most of them were sad War songs. I told Wil how handsome he looked in his uniform. I wished he could come home, so I could show him off. I told him I was so proud of him.

I went almost ten days without a letter from him after our weekend together, so I was getting anxious again. Things changed so quickly with the boys in the Service that any lapse of hearing from them brought the fear that they were being sent out of the States or something had happened to them. It was easy to build things up in my mind and then let them sit there and grow and torture myself with my fears and insecurities. So the letter I wrote February 12th was begging him to write and tell me again that he loved me and only me.

Then I got a letter written February 11th and he said he hadn't written because up until that day he had not missed me as much, and he knew that if he started writing me, he would start missing me so he just didn't write. He said he really enjoyed our weekend together only it did not last long enough. He said he had dreamed about me every night that week. But even so he had been better satisfied than he had since he was sent to Georgia. He wasn't worrying about where they sent him, but he didn't think he could have gone anywhere without seeing me. So I guess the trip was worthwhile because we both seemed to settle down and feel more contented.

He wrote me on Valentine Sunday and had tried to call but could not get through. I quote from that letter:

"Honey, I wish you wouldn't say things like how good I am to you, because I know I am not good to you at all, and when you say such things like that it makes me feel like a heel. I know you don't mean them that way but I can't help feeling like that when I know you are far too good for me. I guess that's why I love you so much because you are so good to me and regardless of how I treat you, you are always the same sweet, little Mary. But don't try to change now because you have spoiled me. Maybe I shouldn't have said that but you have been trying to make me say it for a year."

So, we had each other on a pedestal.
I wrote on Valentine Sunday and told him:

"It is 2:20 pm now. Exactly one year ago this minute we were together. You brought me a box of candy and your new brown suit so I could see it. Do you remember? Seems like all I do now is remember. Guess it's kind of silly but that

is all I have to hold to now until you get back."

How strange that as I re-read these letters, memories are all I have to hold on to in the same time frame in 2005. What would I do without memories?

We had saved some money together, and I was planning to buy a bedroom suite. I had bought and paid for a studio couch by paying so much a week and planned to buy the bedroom suite the same way. In his letter of February 11th he had sent me money with orders to buy some candy or flowers for Valentine and not to put the money in the bank. I always worried about having money saved! I would do without in order to have money on hand for imagined emergencies. I have never gotten away from that habit.

In my letter of February I5th, I had finally gotten his letter of the 11th. I was going to a banquet for the General Shoe Paper Staff on Wednesday night the 17th. I also told him I had another boyfriend. He was 17 and looked about 12 and was employed at General Shoe. He kept pestering me to go to a show with him. He brought me Coca-Colas all the time, and I said I had run out of excuses for not going to a show with him. I finally told him I wasn't dating anyone and he said it wouldn't be a date, that he was just a buddy. I can't even remember his name now.

A letter from Wil written February 16th said he would leave Georgia on February 22nd but had no idea where he would be sent. He said he had another letter from Joyce, but it was not so sappy sweet as the others she wrote. He was not going to answer it, and unless I wanted him to send it to me, he would tear it up. I told him to tear it up, so that was the last of Joyce in our lives. She married shortly after that. He wrote:

"Well, Darling, I've got to close. But remember that I love only you and Honey don't worry".

Telling me not to worry was like trying to re-route a river. My letter to him of the 17th was not as sweet as his. I was upset over not hearing from him more often because I knew they had more time just waiting to be transferred. I had come home from seeing him with good intentions of not being cross with him over anything. But you know about good intentions. So I told him:

"Goodness knows, I don't mind sitting at home and waiting an eternity for you but I would like to know what I am waiting for."

I never stayed cross with him long. On the 17th, I received his letter of the 16th, so I was begging him to forgive me for the letter I wrote the night before.

And the War dragged on.

Mary W. Cordell

31 TRANSFER TO LAMBERT FIELD

Mama, Daddy and Nancye were planning to go to
Jacksonville for Jimmy's graduation the next day. They
would be gone until Monday. Pansy was planning to come
and stay with me and Peggy and Paula. Peggy was nine
and Paula was twelve at the time. I was nearly dead to see
Jimmy before he left Florida but there was no way I could go
because of work and the girls in school.

I wrote Wil Thursday (18th) at lunch, apologizing again if
I had seemed little and hateful because he had not written. I
asked him to please know that it was because I loved him so
very, very much and I was scared that he might stop loving
me. I told him Mama and Daddy and Nancye got off all right.
We had a black woman, who had helped Mama for years
and she was going to stay the weekend with us. The girls
and I were going to the show that night, the ballgames
Friday night and Pansy would be here Saturday night. We
had to walk everywhere we went because the folks took the
car, and I could not drive anyway. But there was always
plenty of company because everyone was walking. It was
really nice meeting and chatting with folks on the street. And
no one was afraid.

I was still trying to decide what to buy with the $10.00
Wil sent me for Valentine's Day. I told him I might buy some
dishes or put it down on some furniture, or I might buy a doll.

140

Even then I loved dolls but never felt I could afford to collect them. (Because Wil never forgot how I yearned to have dolls, I now share my home with over 400 of them.) I wrote him a whole page of how much I loved him and that he was good to me and I loved him, faults and all.

I wrote on the 19th at lunch again. I was still wishing I could have gone to see Jimmy, but I told him I had rather have had the trip to see him. I told him:

"There used to be a time that Jimmy was first with me in everything but no more. I love him better than anything but it's just not like I feel about you"

I had one more letter from Wil when he was still in Georgia. He had called me Saturday night (20th) and then went right to his room and wrote to me. He said he believed I was jealous (he was right) or else I believed he was going to quit me or something He said he guessed he had given me plenty of room to believe that but I should know by now that he would never love anyone else. He admitted that he was jealous also and had been ever since he met me. He said I hadn't given him much reason to be but he was anyway. He wrote:

"That was the reason I asked you a year ago yesterday not to date anyone else. I asked you not to for a long time because I was jealous but I got over most of it. When I left to come down here, that was not the reason I asked you not to. I knew if I told you that I didn't care, you would just think I wanted an excuse to date other girls. I know it wasn't fair to ask you to do it, but I love you so much that I don't care about going out with anyone else and hoped you felt the same way."

And I did. He was packing that night to be sent he didn't know where. We reached an end to Athens, Georgia.

The last week of February dragged on. I wrote every night but held them to mail as soon as I got word where to send them. Wil left Athens on the 22nd with 500 other servicemen. He later wrote that it was a pretty nice trip with only about 275 of the boys drunk. His folks were able to be at the Nashville train station when he passed through, so they were able to visit for a short while. The letter written the 24th and received the 27th told us that he would be stationed at Lambert Field, U. S Naval Station, which was about fifteen miles out of St. Louis, Missouri. That did not seem too far away, and I began making plans to go to see him there. He was really impressed with the base and said it seemed too good to be true, but anything was better than Athens. Since he had so much flight training at Clarksville, they considered him a pilot, so he was ahead of the other officers in flight time. They told him he could fly two hours a day and be through there in two weeks. But he was going to try to stretch it out to six weeks because he liked it there and because he did not know where he would be sent.

He was really happy to be flying again but since he had not flown in four months was somewhat concerned about his skills and afraid he had forgotten. He said they flunked them out of flying for the least reason, but I wasn't worried. Wil was born to fly. I mailed him my letter for the four or five days that I had no address and I received a letter from him written February 28th begging me to write because he missed hearing from me. So began his stay in St. Louis.

America was weary of the War but everyone became reconciled to the fact that we could not win an early victory. Although there was constant fighting in the Pacific, America was steadily fortifying and preparing to invade Japan. Unknown to even the people who worked there we were also developing the atom bomb at Oak Ridge, Tennessee. In Europe, in January of 1943, there was an amphibious landing intended as a flanking operation for the 5th Army at Anzio. The 5th Army was stalled 60 miles away. The landing was accomplished with few casualties. But the 7th Corps commander, General Lucas, had been given orders not to advance from the beachhead if he thought he might get cut off. His decision was to secure and consolidate his beachhead position first, strengthening his supply lines before moving out. Doing this he lost the element of surprise. German Field Marshall Kesselring immediately rushed up two divisions to contain the invasion. Our troops had to dig in and remain in the high ground of the surrounding Alban Hills. They could not advance until the Cassino breakthrough in May – 3 ½ months later. The only news we received was from papers, radio and newsreels at the "picture show". And most of it was old news by the time we heard it. But no one complained. If we had had the discontent, murmurings and criticism that we hear from Americans today, our children and grandchildren would be speaking Japanese.

32 MARCH 1943

I did not hear from Wil as often while he was in St. Louis, but I wrote to him every day. Mama, Daddy and Nancye made the trip to see Jimmy and got back fine with reports that Jimmy was fine. I wrote Wil that I bought a beautiful blue blanket for $8.00 but paid for it myself, putting the money he sent me for Valentine in the bank. We now had $60.00. I thought we were rich. I was also lusting for a pair of golden Navy Wings I saw in Rost Jewelry window and planned to get them as soon as I could. Even at that age, I was making dolls and dressing them, embroidering their dresses and making bonnets. I told Wil I was afraid if he married me he might get disgusted with my dolls. But he never did. I think he loved them too because he certainly bought me a lot of them when we finally retired and settled down, years later.

The first week of March was a tragic week for my family. Aunt Julia (Mama's sister) and her husband lived in Cleveland, Ohio with their two younger daughters. Uncle Jess was an engineer on the railroad. On February 28th, he was killed in a train accident. Their son, Howard, was in the Army and had just gone back after being home on furlough. That was the third accidental death in my mother's family in 2 ½ years. She had a large family, and as Uncle Jess was brought here for burial we had a week or ten days of lots of company. Aunt Julia and the girls moved to Pulaski shortly after that and were here until after the War.

The next letter I got from Wil from St. Louis contained a charred piece of a parachute. One of his buddies had crashed with another Navy plane, killing both pilots. I really needed to hear that. I received two more pieces of parachutes while he was in St. Louis. He was flying every day, and he wrote that it was sometimes 30 degrees below zero at 3000 feet. His group was really trained strenuously to fly, and we knew later that they were being trained to be ready when we invaded Japan. Wil was telling me again how much he enjoyed the two weeks in my life. What I wouldn't give for just a few days of that right now. He also wrote:

"I love you so much that anything you do is all right with me."

March did not offer much to write about. Aunt Julia and the girls went back to Cleveland on the 9th, and things settled down again. Daddy got the bug to buy a farm. He and Mama always loved the country. So we spent the next few Sunday afternoons driving to farms that were for sale. Some were desirable land but no house, some a fair house but no electricity. I would breathe a sigh of relief when one was not suitable because I would have had to have a room alone in town so I could work.

Nancye had her sixth birthday on March 7, 1943. I wrote that you would have thought she was the only child in the world to be six, the way we carried on. Daddy and I gave her a new coat.

On March 8, Wil wrote that he had flown that day in the 30 degree below zero weather. He wanted me to plan to come to see him as soon as I could. He had to have his hair cut so he cut it flat on top. There went his beautiful wavy hair, and he became a tough pilot.

During this time, everyone was wondering and worrying about John Alton because no one was hearing from him.

On March 10th, I wrote Wil that Jimmy was trying to

decide if he would apply for gunnery school or officers' training. He would be leaving Jacksonville in May, and we were praying he would qualify for further training. I told Wil we got our "Victory Garden" dug up that day and planted potatoes, onions, mustard and lettuce and would get the rest of it planted the next week.

I wrote on the 11th and told him :

"I wonder just what I lived for before I started planning on our home and everything. If we could be together, I wouldn't care if we just had one room."

I told him to be careful and to be sure to come back to me.

In my letter of March 13th I wrote that Burt Furniture had called to tell me they had received a bedroom suite but it was $110.00, so I didn't feel that I should bite off that much. I had bought a cedar chest so I could give Mama's back to her. I think the cedar chest cost about $16.00.

By mid March, Pansy and I were planning to go to St. Louis the first weekend in April. So I was getting excited. We would go by train, leaving Nashville at 8pm Friday night and arriving in St. Louis by 9am Saturday. I told Wil to find Pansy a good-looking cadet so she could have a good time. I was wondering why I wasn't getting more letters from him.

In the letter of March 15th I was upset about the amount of work I had to do at the factory. I was training a new girl for the office in addition to Roberta. I had been offered a job at the Mines at $110.00 a month but was not going to take it.

I had decided if I could not be with Wil after he got his Wings, I was not going to stay in Pulaski. I said there must be somewhere more interesting than this place.

Wil also wrote on March 15th. He had gone into St. Louis the past weekend and had tried to call but could not get through to me. He did talk to Pansy. He told her to plan to come April 3 and he was hoping I could come also. He said he had a good time in St. Louis. It felt good to be in a big city again. He said St. Louis was the fifth largest city in the U. S. and said there were more saloons than anything else. He wrote he didn't think he had ever missed me more than he did the last Sunday because the weather was so pretty, and he had dreamed about me every night that week. That news made me feel better because I was wondering about the good time in St. Louis without me.

On March 17th, I went to a reporter's meeting and banquet. I was on the staff of the General Shoe Newspaper, and we had a meeting once a month. Roberta had spent the night before with me, and we went to a show—what else? We saw GIRL TROUBLE and I thought it was real "cute". Mama and Daddy were at Frankewing because Grandpa Whitlock and "Miss" Ethel were moving there from Prospect. They planned to open a store there, and Daddy was putting up shelves. The woman who had the farm for sale had backed out of selling, so Daddy still didn't have his farm. And I still had a room with them.

At the factory, we had been pushing for a raise. The work was piling up and getting harder and the office force was still getting only 40 cents an hour. (Can you imagine anyone today working for that?} We were asking for 45 cents an hour but the factory claimed they could not pay that. Then they hired a girl and paid her 45 cents an hour. So we all threatened to quit. I wrote Wil that if I didn't like the work I was doing so well, I would quit anyway. I really did like the office work. I told him that helped me to understand how he felt about flying.

I wrote him that my letters sounded as if I was writing to a stranger, but I was getting such a few letters from him I was beginning to feel like we were strangers. Then when I got a letter from him the whole world looked rosy again, and I would think how silly I was to worry. I wrote Wil that there was a man at the factory I had known for a long time. He had appointed himself as my "confidante and adviser". He had been married for three years, but he told me he was in love with a girl who jilted him before he married this other girl. In talking about the girl who jilted him, he told me did not think it was possible to ever get over your first love. So I told Wil I hoped I was the first person he ever really loved. In a later letter, he answered that he agreed with my friend and I was his first real love. He said he thought he loved Joyce, but if that was love, he didn't know how to describe what he felt for me.

On March 17th he wrote wanting us to come the third of April, but he would not get much time off that weekend. They had taken away some of their liberty, so the only free time he would have would be on Sunday afternoon. That letter also burst a balloon or two for me because he wrote:

"Darling, you said if you couldn't come to me this Fall, you would leave Pulaski. I certainly don't want to tear down your hopes but there isn't one chance in a hundred that you can come to me. If I am lucky enough to get through OK, I won't get to stay anywhere long. If I get the Fighter Squadron, then I'll go straight across. You know I want you more than anything else, but it's just got to be that way. In fact, I have wanted you so badly this week that I have been thinking about resigning and going into the Army Air Corps. The best friend I have up here is going to get kicked out tomorrow for going on night flight while drunk. He called the Army Air Corps today and they told him they would be glad to get him. He wants me to go with him and it sure is a temptation. If I hadn't already gone through so much hell, I would quit in a minute, but I am practically half way through, so I don't know what to do. I guess I'll stay in this for a while longer if I don't get kicked out or something. I wouldn't be surprised at it any time. That is the feeling of everyone here."

There was lots of frustration for everyone then, but as it worked out it was much better that he stayed with the Navy and then went into the Marine Corps.

33 MARCH-APRIL 1943

On the night of March 18,1943, we were all at Grandpa's in Frankewing, and I hung pictures, arranged furniture and washed and put away dishes. I was still planning to go to St. Louis on April 3rd since I had not received his letter of the17th. I wrote to him after getting home after 11 p.m. that night, so it wasn't much of a letter.

He wrote on the 19th and said he had some time because the weather was too bad to fly. He had heard from Donald. He was in California getting ready to go overseas. That was the letter in which he referred to my "confidant's" philosophy about first love. He said further that if I were the 100th girl he had loved, I would still be the only one he loved or ever would. He was looking forward to our visit in April.

In my letter to him after receiving the above mentioned letter, I told him I had really been blue all day, especially after getting his letter of the 17th. I was disappointed that his time the weekend of the 3rd would be so limited. And I was feeling like we were never going to have our time together. I was wishing I had married him when he wanted me to. Nothing about love makes sense, does it?

By March 25th, things looked better. Wil had found out he would be free the entire weekend of April 17th, so Pansy and I changed our plans to go that weekend. I wrote Wil I had gotten a box of candy that day from an inspector who came down once a month, and I did his typing. He had left money the month before for someone to buy me candy. He was a 50 year old bachelor, so I got a lot of teasing about that.

In that letter, I was the aggressor. I told Wil even if he had only two days leave I wanted to get married before he went overseas. I told him he could use my letter to prove I asked him. I told him if he did not marry me before he left, so help me, I would forget all about him while he was gone (fat chance of that!).

My married "confidante" at work was continuing to give me advice. I wrote:

"I can't even go upstairs to take up a report that he doesn't stop me to talk over the situation. I don't know why his interest but I'm really afraid his wife is going to pull my hair out sometimes. And believe me, I didn't so much as wink at him. But seriously, he thinks I'm so wonderful that you should come right home and marry me. Silly, isn't he? And I guess this sounds silly telling it to you, but how do you get rid of someone who you like okay but they bore you anyway?"

On Saturday, March 27, Mama and I went to town, and I bought a new winter coat, bright red. I was walking on air because our trip the 16th was going forward in planning, and Pansy could go that weekend. A sad note on that day was that a truckload of our boys were taken to boot camp. James Alton Pigg was among them, and we all felt so sorry for "Uncle" Bryant. I wrote there were over 100 people there to see them off and it was a sad occasion. I also wrote Wil that the three little sisters had just come in. They had played with some little boys all afternoon. I wrote:

"I believe they'll all be married before I am at the rate they're going. I guess they can take their time and then beat me. Ha!"

I wrote on Sunday the 28th that we had spent all

afternoon looking at farms again. I cannot recall why Daddy never got his big farm, but there was always some drawback. After the War he did buy 13 acres at the edge of town and built a house, actually two houses, there.

Jimmy was still in Jacksonville, getting further training as a Navigator. He was hoping for a furlough when he completed that training. By this time, Wil was training with the Marines. He wrote:

"My opinion of a Marine is rapidly growing worse. They put a Marine Captain in charge of our regiment and he sure is a pain in the neck. But I haven't seen a Marine yet that wasn't. He made the most conceited talk the day he took over that I've ever heard. His name is Kolp and every time a cadet meets another, he says "Heil Kolp," and gives the German salute. I'm just waiting for the day that he sees it. Maybe he will realize he's not so important."

Wil had heard from Jimmy, and Jimmy told him he was dating an 18 year old girl who had to slip out to meet him because her parents would not let her date servicemen. But nothing ever came of it.

April of 1943 was pretty exciting. After much back and forth chit-chat, it was decided Pansy and I would go to see Wil in St. Louis the weekend of the 16th – 18th. I was walking on air for two weeks. Even my Daddy thought I should go because he was afraid we would count on Wil getting a few days furlough and then, like in Athens, it would be canceled. Daddy was always in my corner, anyway. And I adored him.

The first of the month, Mama and I were busy at nights and weekends updating the living room. I covered two chairs and made draperies. We got a new carpet and did Spring cleaning. My days were so busy at work, and then we would work every night so I lost even more weight.

On April 1st, Wil wrote to confirm he was supposed to be off the weekend of the 16th and wanted us to come. He was still fussing about the Marine Captain Kolp and the changes he had made. Discipline was a lot tighter under Marine control, but in spite of that, he had signed up with the Marine Corps. He did that because it gave him a better chance at being a fighter pilot or a dive-bomber. He was afraid if he stayed in the Navy they would make him an instructor, and that was not what he wanted. At that time, Wil had become very close to his Dad by way of letters. Wil could always write his feelings for people better than he could verbalize them. I really loved Gram, so I understood both of them.

On April 3rd, I wrote that Peggy (9years old) had a party and I was supposed to entertain the children. They all wanted to go walking with their girls or boys and play drug store. I wrote:

"I really don't know what the younger generation is coming to."

I also wrote I was listening to the radio and the Duke of Paducah was on giving advice on courtship. I thought he had some pretty good points. I was telling him about the boys he knew here who had left for the service. James Alton Pigg was in Massachusetts, Cecil Brock was in California, Stooge (James Ed) Holt was called up to see the draft board so Helen was crying and upset over that. Before the letter was finished I wrote that someone on the Grand Ole Opry was singing "Time Can Never Change My Love For You" and I wished they would hurry up and hush as it was a sad song.

They were sad times, so many families separated, some of the boys never coming back and some would come back so damaged and changed. But America struggled on and worked hard, little complaining but a determination to win the War and have peace on Earth. And I was wishing the 16th would hurry up and come.

34 TRIP TO ST. LOUIS

Nancye had the measles the first week of April. It was a new strain, and the doctors were afraid everyone would take them even if they had had the old kind. So I was scared to death I would get them and not be able to go to St. Louis. But that did not happen, and plans were progressing.

Wil's letter of April 4th was a blue letter. They had two plane crashes. One boy was killed. The other was not expected to live, and if he did he would be blind and crippled. Wil knew him real well. His girl was coming to St. Louis, and the boy had told Wil they were going to slip off and get married. She came, but she had not been able to see the boy. Wil was really upset for her, and he was wondering how things would end for us. He said:

"It seems like this War or fate or whatever you call it is taking all and giving nothing."

He was almost through with his flying there but would have to have six more weeks training for ground school. He wrote:

"I sure hope I can get one or two days off before I leave here. I guess you know why. In case you don't, there's a certain girl down your way I want to add a Mrs. to her name.

I think I had better do it while I am still alive and well. Don't you agree? Darling, I keep missing and wanting you more every day. Something has got to be done. It just can't go on much longer. We are due for a break sometime."

It really bothered him when his buddies got killed.

A letter from Pansy on the 5th said they had a cable from John Alton, and he had landed safely somewhere in Europe. He had gone across the ocean on a ship was the reason we went so long without hearing. That just increased our worry about him.

I lived with the fear of Wil being in a plane crash, and when I got his letter about the two pilots who had "cracked up", I wrote:

"Darling, that is why I have decided that the present is all that is important because the future is so uncertain. It's funny that I should wait until it's too late to decide that but I guess I never knew just how much I cared and how much I was going to miss you until you left in November. I wrote you a long letter two weeks ago trying to explain it to you but I tore it up because words just cannot express how you feel about some things. Maybe sometime I can tell you how I feel about your being gone and us not being married. I just wonder if you feel that one night could help you face anything that might happen and without some time together you just couldn't take those things that might happen. I guess I should tear this letter up also because unless you have felt the same way it will sound silly. But I know what I mean. I know what I want now more than anything else in the world, whether anyone else knows or not. Darling, much as I hate to, I have to face the fact that there are possibilities that you won't come back. I believe and pray that you will but no one can be sure. And because of that, that's why I hope that fate or whatever it is will give us a little time together because only in that way can we know that we really belonged."

Isn't it funny that we felt the only way we could really

belong to each other was to be married? And now our moral society would think we were crazy not to just be together, married or not. But that never even occurred to us. And we were always so glad we waited.

I kept writing although there was not much going on at home at that time and even though it was only a few more days until we would be together. On Saturday, April 10th, I dug up a spot and planted a flower garden and then made a dress. The next night I made a pair of shorts for Paula. We had an old treadle machine but I could throw things together and have them ready to wear in an afternoon or night. Now I wonder if they were even fit to wear. I had made real good grades in Home Economics, and, of course, necessity is the mother of invention. But I could not make a garment in one day now if I had to.

One other happening – Peggy was playing ball on Sunday, the 11th, and injured her arm. We thought it was broken but it wasn't. She was always getting injured. When she was crawling and we had the little coal grates for heat, she crawled up close to the fire and some way got her head hung in the grate We had trouble getting her out, and she still has a scar at the back of her head. Another time she managed to run her arm through the wringer of our Maytag washing machine. It was mashed flat but she was so young her bones were flexible enough that nothing was broken. She later became a nurse and left her klutzy ways behind. As for my making shorts for Paula, it would have been a major upheaval in the family if I had even mentioned wearing shorts when I was twelve years old.

On April 11th, Wil asked me in his letter if I would want to marry him if he could get just one day off. I wrote back that I would marry him if we only had an hour. But I still did not want him to jeopardize getting his Wings.

So we made the trip to St. Louis. I took a bus to Nashville, and Pansy and I boarded the train the night of the 16th. I do not remember that night on the train. I know it was crowded, but I was so tired and so excited I think I slept all the way. It was packed with Service men and we were two of only about fifteen other women on the train. We got to

St. Louis about 8 a.m. and went to the hotel where Wil had reserved our room. He joined us about noon. I wish I could remember what we did that afternoon and night, but I can't. He went back to the base late that night. I do remember he was knocking on our door before we were up and dressed the next morning. We had all day together. According to both of our letters after, it was a wonderful day together. Pansy has said several times that she really felt she was in the way, but I was happy she was there. We left St. Louis at 8 p.m. on Sunday night. The train was very crowded again with the "boys". They were seated in the aisles on their suitcases. Pansy was very popular with everyone but I was not interested in their attentions. She finally went to sit with a soldier who made room for her, and I was able to sleep most of the way. We arrived in Nashville Monday morning and I caught the No 3 train on home, arriving late afternoon. I wrote:

"I can never, never tell you how much I enjoyed this weekend. I almost cried when I got to Pulaski. I think I hated this place worse than I have ever hated anything. But I came home, cleaned up, and went on to work so I feel a little better now."

Of course, what private time we had in St. Louis was spent planning to get married. We were going to get married if he could get just two days off before being transferred. I even called Mr. Abernathy, the County Court Clerk, and pretended I was calling for a couple I knew. He told me to come by the next day and he would give me the papers the "couple" would have to fill out and that the "boy" could get his blood test ahead of time wherever he was. I sent Wil his papers and planned to get my blood test when I knew for sure what we could do. We planned on telling no one what we were going to do. But I had to talk to Mama. At first she would not even talk about it until I told her we were trying to plan it so we could be married here in Pulaski. Then she seemed a lot more interested. She told Daddy and as usual he was willing to do anything to help us. So I was making big plans. We were going to wait until we were sure before telling the Cordells. I made several different plans. I would have the license when he got here, and we would be married in the church right after Sunday morning worship.

Hope springs eternal, and his letters sounded as excited as mine over what we planned to do. I sent the papers by Special Delivery. It cost me thirteen cents. I also talked to the license office (pretending again it was for another couple). They said we could get a license on Sunday morning. I am sure I did not fool anyone with my fabricated fictitious couple because everyone in Pulaski knew everyone else's business.

But I was walking on air feeling that nothing would go wrong this time.

35 TENTATIVE WEDDING PLANS

Our house was in an uproar anyway that week because Mama had decided the living room looked so nice she wanted the rest of the rooms painted. So that took the painters a week or so. Roberta was staying with us that week because her little sister had the measles, and Roberta was afraid she would take them. I was glad to have her because I was a nervous wreck over wedding plans. I only weighed 98 lbs. by that time, and Wil wasn't too happy over that. Both of us kept assuring the other of our undying love and that we could wait three more months if we had to. And because of so many past disappointments, I still delayed getting my blood test.

I found out our preacher, Bro. Fox, would be gone the Sunday we had planned. Daddy said he and Mama could drive us to Murfreesboro Sunday morning and let Bro. Elmer Smith marry us. He was a good friend. Daddy said we could then go to Nashville to the Cordells. He had not met all of the family at that time. I was not getting any objections from my family, and I had not told the Cordells. Wil wanted me to write them as soon as I knew what we could do. I wrote Wil that I guessed Evelyn would feel hurt that I didn't write her about our plans, but I told him I wasn't asking anyone's permission this time. I told him:

"The way I look at it, they'll get over it in two or three weeks anyway."

But I did keep telling Wil not to get in any trouble by coming so far from the base.   April 24, 1943, my twentieth birthday, was on Saturday, and I was not even up to going to town with Mama. Paula had two girls to spend the night before with her, and they had gone to the Sub-Deb dance at the Coca-Cola plant. I told Wil Mama was pulling her hair out over it, but she let her go anyway. I was never allowed to dance, but Paula had a mind of her own. We were getting ready to have all of Daddy's family the next day for a family reunion. Nancye had gone to an Easter egg hunt that afternoon. Two little boys gave Peggy a box of candy, a bottle of perfume and pin for her lapel and six cents, all for Easter. I wonder why six cents?

While they were there that Sunday, a bomber plane flew over and circled our house about ten times. The family teased me that it was Wil, but I told them if it was him, he would have jumped out and stayed with me a while.

Time was running out for the proposed wedding plans, but I was not hearing from Wil. He wrote on the 27th that he didn't write because he still could not tell me anything for certain, but it did not look promising that he could get away. He knew for sure he could not come the next weekend as planned but possibly could make it in two weeks. If so, he thought he could get here in time to be married Saturday evening. If so, that would really be better. They were really busy, trying to get in the training needed before leaving St. Louis. He wrote:

"Darling, I don't see why you keep worrying about me changing my mind. You should know that I don't want to change it. I think I've looked forward to our marriage a lot longer than you have. If I intended to back out I would have done it long before now. Honey, if you just keep loving me as much as I love you then I'll be happy.

There is nothing that can change the way I feel about you."

So I had to be content with that and wait a little longer. We were so restricted to restrictions. It was very frustrating, but we were not alone. So many were in the same situations.

April 1943 came to a close, and nothing had changed. We did have the visit in St. Louis but being together only made us more anxious to be together for a longer time. But we survived.

May, 1943 began with the hope that Wil could get a furlough before being transferred. But, I tried to dampen my excitement because we had been disappointed so many times. I was so happy I had made no announcements in April, so there was nothing to take back.

On May 2nd , we all drove to Elkmont after church and I drove the car from Ardmore to Elkmont. We visited Uncle Ben's family. He was Mama's brother. Their daughter, Anna Roe, was a dear cousin, and we were very close. Her boyfriend came, so I was jealous that they were still together. But he was younger than we were and still not drafted.

I wrote Wil that Daddy had bought a new suit and was so proud of it that he had to model it for us. As usual, he had a cigarette in his mouth and an ash fell and burned a minute hole in it. He was so upset that we got tickled. It was tiny so no real harm done.

We had heard from Jimmy, and he was headed for the West Coast for sure with no hope of a furlough. Mama was really sick over it, and I was so upset over not seeing him again.

At this point in time, the coal miners went on strike. It was a very unpatriotic thing to do in wartime. We were all wishing President Roosevelt would put them all in the Army and send them straight to the front. I'm sure the strike was not allowed to go on very long.

In Wil's letter of May 3rd, he was still planning to come in two weeks. He had sent me another fountain pen because I had lost my good one. That was before we had ballpoint pens and that is probably one reason our letters are still readable after 62 years.

On May 4th, I wrote that nothing was happening in Pulaski except that Nancye fell into the fish pond next door, so we had to pet her for a couple of hours. She was such a cute little girl. News from Nashville was that Clifford had fallen from a train and was in the hospital, but he soon recuperated. He was drafted when they started drafting fathers, about 1944. He spent quite a while in Europe.

Wil was still leaving it up to me to write and tell his folks what our plans were. But I was reluctant to do that because I felt the plans would get changed as usual. I finally wrote to them. I received a sweet letter from Mother Cordell assuring me that whatever we worked out would be fine with them.

On May 6th, Mama got up and announced she was going to see Jimmy before he left. Daddy could get away to take her, so she left on the bus that afternoon. That was so unusual for Mama, but I think she would have walked rather than not see him again. I felt the same way but I had to work, and someone had to take care of the girls. I do not know how I managed but I worked, fed the family, and kept the house going. I felt it was worth it because Jimmy was so happy she was coming. She stayed in Jacksonville from Friday until the next Tuesday. She got home on Wednesday. She told me to tell Wil she would be back in time for our wedding. Everyone was very encouraging but I think we all knew that there would be no wedding. Things were just too hectic and plans oft went astray. But hope kept us going.

36 PENSACOLA POSTPONEMENT

During the first week of May, 1943, Dad Cordell was unable to work due to illness. He lost a lot of weight, and he had yellow jaundice with a blocked gall bladder. The doctor thought he would need surgery. So Mother Cordell had the doctor write to St. Louis to see if Wil could get a leave. When Wil wrote me the 9th, he was pretty sure he could get a leave. His folks wanted us to come to Nashville to be married but that would have been too public, trying to keep everything a secret but more and more people were being involved. The preacher there, Bro Baird, sent word he would be happy to tie the knot. The promise of a leave would mean more time at home, so it really began to look like luck was on our side. I made my dress to be married in. I wish I could remember what it looked like. I could tell by Wil's letter that he was still worried that getting married might get him kicked out as a pilot.

On Monday, May 10th, I wrote Wil how busy I had been with Mama gone. I had worked all day, came home and cooked supper, cleaned the kitchen, helped Dad to pull weeds in the garden, took a bath, washed some things and rolled my hair. I was down to 95 pounds. I was thinking I would see a doctor even if I did not need the blood test.

Aunt Gladys, Uncle Coleman and Paul Wayne had spent the night before with us, and she helped me get everyone off to work and school that morning. I wrote Wil I did not know how a family ever made it without their Mother.

Mama was home in time to go to Prayer Meeting that Wednesday night, and after reading Mother Cordell's letter, Mama decided it would be better to be married in Nashville by Bro. Baird because she and Daddy could go with us, and that way the Cordells could be included. One thing Wil and I were blessed with...our families were so compatible.

But as usual, "best laid plans of mice and men oft go awry," once more our plans were put on hold. In a letter from Wil, written May 13th the news was that they told him that morning that he would not get his leave. He would have to be in St. Louis that Sunday to get ready to leave Monday morning. They had decided that since Dad Cordell was not in the hospital he was not very sick. Wil said he just did not say anything because he knew he would lose his temper and say too much. He was really down and out but was still hopeful of getting a few days before going overseas. He wrote:

"But, Darling, if it happens I don't get home anymore, remember that I love you now and I always will."

I cried half the night when I received that letter. But Life dragged on, Dad Cordell recovered and things sort of settled down until further developments. We were all so sad then. Jimmy was on his way to the West Coast, and we were sure he would be sailing soon. Wil was being transferred, but we did not know where he was going. He still had two or three more months of training but we were afraid he would be too far for us to visit. The next letter I received from him he was in Pensacola, Florida. He said it was like a luxury resort compared to the other places he had been. He could walk to the beach from his barracks and he spent his spare time swimming and sunning on the beach. But he was to be sent somewhere to an outlying field for two or three weeks to fly. He thought it would take about four months to finish up at Pensacola. He was still hoping to get accepted as a fighter pilot. He wanted me to plan to come to see him in

Pensacola when he got back there. Gerald Green, from Nashville, was at Pensacola also and he and Wil wanted his girl friend and me to come together. That would be great, but Gerald was sent to another base, so we never got to do that. Gerald and Wil remained good friends. Gerald was killed In the War and we named our son, Gerald Dykes, after him.

I had accumulated four or five letters to mail to Wil as soon as I got his new address. So began another period of waiting and hoping.

On May 21st, Wil wrote that they were supposed to have a pressure test the next morning (Saturday) to determine what altitude they could tolerate. That would tell them what kind of plane they could fly. He still hoped for fighters. He said he wanted to see me worse than he ever had, and he hoped he would never again be as disappointed as he was about not getting home. His folks did manage to see him for a few minutes when the train to Pensacola stopped in Nashville. I'm sure they all went to the station to see him.

On the 23rd, Wil still had not had time for my letters to catch up with him. He wrote:

"Darling, you don't know how much I miss you and your letters. It doesn't seem like the day is right unless I get a letter from you. I guess that is why I want to see you so much, because I haven't heard from you in almost a week. Well, I will start flying again tomorrow. I sure am glad of it, too, because it will make the time fly a lot faster. I certainly want these next few months to pass as quickly as possible. They can't pass too soon for me. My instructor in St. Louis heard me say that and he said I was having the time of my life right now and just didn't realize it. I told him he didn't know what I had waiting for me at the end of all this. When I started this training it was the Wings I was working for but now it's different. I'm still working for the Wings because that's when I can have you and I'd rather have you than the Wings but I hope I can get both."

He wrote on the 24th that he had been flying that day

and it was great. The planes were a lot faster there. But reality was setting in. He would only get one day off in every eight days, so I could make no plan to visit him. He wrote four pages trying to tell me about the choices of which plane to fly. However, he said they would let them ask and then would assign them where the Marines wanted them to be. He thought he might ask for patrol boats, and then he would probably be stationed where I could be with him. I would have loved that, but I encouraged him to ask for what he liked. If he had to fly, I wanted him to be happy doing it.

I had gone to Nashville to spend the weekend with the Cordells and had a real nice time. They were my family now. Paula went with me that weekend. I wrote that Evelyn and family and Clifford and family came to see me while we were there. I told him the kids were as sweet as ever. That would have been Denny, Wayne and Bobbi Jean. I really loved the children. Dad Cordell looked bad, but he was planning to go back to work.

On May 24th, I wrote Wil that Jimmy was now in San Diego, California. They had been issued rifles and helmets, but he was going to try to get more training before having to go overseas. I told Wil I either had to stand up on the bus coming from Nashville or sit by a soldier so I sat and wished I hadn't. Then there was no room for me to get up and stand again. But I told him I won round one, and he was pretty nice after that. My point was that the soldier said I must really be in love with someone. I guess I didn't even have to tell anyone I was in love. I just mentioned Wil's name and they knew.

I was still such a baby in so many ways – the love of dolls and small children. And I had bought three baby turtles in Nashville and had them in a bowl in my room. I told Wil I could watch them all night they were so cute. My cousin, Malcolm Jones, was home on furlough. He was in the Army and ready to go overseas.

Wil was writing more often as he had more time in Pensacola. And he was getting my letters. I was beginning to accept that we would not be married until he had his Wings. I always felt that things happened for the best. I was seeing Joyce at that time at church and different places. She was wearing a small diamond on her right hand. I wished she would quit wearing it. Not really.

I wrote on May 27th that I was spending the night with Roberta. They lived on a country road up a hollow, and it was so quiet and lonely there. They did not have electricity so I was writing by the light of an oil lamp. Her brother, Jimmy, was in the Navy and home on furlough. He had just finished a course in welding and would leave the next weekend for California and then overseas. Everyone was so sad and so worried. Mama had lost ten pounds and went to the doctor. He told her it was her nerves that were shot. But we all knew that she was just so worried about Jimmy.

Aunt Julia and her girls moved from Cleveland to a house she bought in Pulaski the last week in May. She and the girls had been at our house waiting for their furniture to arrive. Mama's house was like living in a hotel, we almost always had guests that stayed while they waited for their life to be regained again. My mother never seemed to mind and if Daddy did, he never complained about it

37 JUNE 1943

In a letter to Wil on May 28th, I had good news. Jimmy was selected to train as a Navigator, so he would be in California for several months. He was the only one in his squadron who didn't ship out. Never underestimate the power of prayer.

Wil wrote on May 30th that he had a letter from Thomas and Sarah Hamlett, and they were expecting a baby. That was the couple we ran around with and went to Athens, Alabama to get married; only Wil and I backed out. Wil said they were getting a pretty good start on us.

I wrote Wil on the 30th that I had helped cook breakfast for the soldiers at the USO that Sunday morning but did not bring any of them home with me for dinner. I told him I just couldn't seem to care if one of them looked at me or not. I went to the Jones family reunion after church just so I could be with Malcolm and Laura Dew.

I had a holiday on the 31st (Memorial Day). I did write to Wil that day, and the letter is in the box, but it got wet or something and is unreadable. I'm sure there was nothing in it of importance.

And so we made it to June, 1943. On June 1st Daddy went on a fishing trip with two other men to be gone until Friday. I told Wil they carried a boat, cots, blankets and enough food to feed an army. Daddy was as excited as a little kid. He really worked hard at the station, so we were happy he could get away.

Wil was flying formation in Florida. That sounded a lot more dangerous to me, but he was enjoying it. My cousin, Mary Phillips Daly, wanted to make the trip to Pensacola with me, so I started making plans for that. She would go only if Wil could find her a Cadet who liked to dance. She was 22, and I told him she was cute as a bug and a lot of fun. So I began to plan for that trip.

A few interesting things happened in June. From June 5-8th, a minor fight between sailors and Mexican "Pachucos" wearing Zoot Suits led to the Los Angeles Zoot Suit riots in which uniformed sailors, marines and soldiers rampaged through the streets of downtown Los Angeles, beating first those wearing Zoot Suits and then anyone with dark skin. The police stood by and then moved in and arrested the victims. The City Council adopted a resolution declaring that the wearing of a Zoot Suit was a misdemeanor, but the rioting did not end until military authorities declared Los Angeles off limits.

On June 10th, W-2 Day, the Withholding Tax Act was passed by Congress providing a "pay-as-you-go" tax. On June 20th, there was a riot in Detroit that left twenty-five blacks and nine whites dead. This was sparked by a false rumor that a black man had raped a white woman.

Meanwhile on the War front the Royal Air Force and the U. S. 8th Air Force delivered four massive raids against Hamburg, Germany, killing 43,000 people and injuring many more. These raids introduced what was known as firestorms. The searing fires the bombs produced created an air column 2½ miles high and nearly two miles in diameter. It produced tornado-like winds that spread the fires with uncontrollable speed. These raids and others cost almost 160,000 Allied flyers their lives during the War.

Daddy got back from his fishing trip all right and had a wonderful time. Paula had been somewhere all week, but she came home so we were all settled in again.

I wrote Wil on June 4th that is was really getting hot here. I had helped Daddy hoe the garden that night and had taken my bath. But was so hot I was thinking about taking another one. I didn't see how we would stand the factory during the hot summer. There was no air conditioning then. I was not feeling well and could not gain any weight.

We had heard from Jimmy, and he would be flying in a Transport plane as a Navigator when he finished training. Our meeting was starting in a week at church, and we had been selected to keep the preacher at our house. Our house was still like a hotel. I wanted Evelyn and Allen to come for a visit during her vacation. I always felt free to invite anyone I wanted because Mama did not seem to mind.

In my letter of Sunday, June 6th, I said we were all in the yard under the shade trying to keep cool. Daddy had a cot out there, and he was asleep. I can still see all of us in my mind. Memories are one of the puzzles of our life. I wrote that I had heard Joyce got married, so that ended that aggravation.

I still wanted to know when Mary Phillips and I could come to Pensacola.

On June 6th, Wil wrote from the outlying field where he had been sent for flying. He finished formation flying that day and then had a week of ground school before being sent back to the main base. He would find out in three more weeks what type plane he would fly in battle. If he got Fighter or Dive Bomber, it would take eight more weeks; P-T boat would take six more weeks. He said Denny had a birthday coming up on the 16th, but he could only send a card because he was not able to go to town from where he was.

On the 7th, I wrote that I guessed Joyce was really married because Mama saw her and some boy in a car with lots of clothes and things in it. I wrote:

"I certainly hope they will be happy because if it hadn't been for Joyce I might never have met you. Sometimes I wonder what I lived for before I met you. Everything I do, think or feel centers around you. It is as if you are here all the time. Everything I do I wonder how you would feel about it. Even when I am doing something else I am thinking of

you."

How little my feelings have changed after all these years. I still think of him all the time.

With so much rationing during the War, food was also on the meager list and we had to have stamps for everything we needed. So even about two blocks from the Square in Pulaski, my Daddy had a garden, a chicken house with chickens, a pen for white rabbits, which he raised for food and not for petting. Mama had a cow called Bessie and Bessie had a calf. So we were never hungry and I guess it was one reason people loved to visit us as we always had good fresh food and milk and plenty of whipping cream and butter. We had an acre of land where the two story house we rented was located so no one thought anything about our mini-farm.

But disaster struck and Daddy's chicken house burned the first week of June. It caused a bit of excitement. Daddy got singed a little getting the chickens out. He started right away building a new one.

All was well at our house again and life went on.

38 SUMMER WHIRLWIND

On June 14th, Wil wrote he had just been too busy to write. He was transferred back from the outlying field to the base. He would be at the main base for two or three more weeks of instrument flying. Then he would go back to an outlying field for squadron training. That would take six to eight weeks more, and he should be through training. They had a pressure test that day to see how they would fare at 40,000 feet. That would decide which type plane he would qualify for. If they failed the test,, they would get PT boats or scout planes. He said he passed. He asked for Fighters first then Torpedo Bombing, PT boats, instructor and scout, in that order. He wound up as a Torpedo Bomber pilot.

He was feeling that I shouldn't try to come to Pensacola because of his schedule. There was only one decent hotel, and it stayed full. But he was still trying to figure out a way.

On June l5th, I wrote that our church meeting was going on, but we got out of keeping the preacher. Frances Hollins, from Gallatin, was visiting me, and we fed three preachers for both meals on Sunday the l3th. I was worrying if I could keep working at the factory because of the heat and my lack of energy. I was so worried about Wil flying so much. The husband of one of Anna Roe's friends was a pilot, and he was killed that week.

I wrote that Jimmy was enjoying the school, and his

grades were sixth in his class. We also had a letter from Bill Maultsby who had joined the Marines with Jimmy. He was put into a special unit because of his height and was already in the South Pacific. I think that was about the last letter we had from Bill. He was killed in a battle for one of the islands.

My letters became pretty boring those hot nights. Frances went home on Tuesday (16th) so I was lonesome again. I went to the meeting every night which was tiring me out. On Friday night, the 28th, we had our first blackout. I had to write late that night, but I told Wil I sort of enjoyed the 15 or 20 minutes of darkness and total quiet. It was really weird for the whole town to be dark and silent. But no bombs were dropped!

Wil's letter of the 19th quelled any hopes I had of going to see him in Pensacola. But he thought he might get 21 days leave when he got his Wings, which should be the last of August. They were canceling the weekend leaves mostly because so many pilots were losing their lives, and they thought it might be because of the weekends in town. I think by that time I expected plans to be changed, and the thought of 21 days leave was wonderful.

On Sunday, June 20th, our meeting was still on. Paula was baptized this week. I was hoping that would put an end to her wanting to go to the dances. Daddy, the girls and I played croquet all afternoon, and then we ordered ice cream and had a party. My Mother and Daddy really were good parents. I had not heard from Wil in a week, and I always complained and worried when he couldn't write. I lived for his letters. I told him there was a white bedspread at the store where Aunt Jim worked. It was $8.00, but she could buy it for me for $5.00. I told her I might never get to use the things I had bought, but she said they would be good memories.

Anna Roe came to visit this week and go to church. She had promised an 18 year old boy she would marry him. She was almost 21, and she had changed her mind. She didn't know how to tell the boy she did not love him. She wanted Wil to send me a special delivery letter telling her what to do. I was feeling too sorry for the boy to give her good advice.

On June 22nd, I wrote Wil that we were in church and Uncle Gilbert and Aunt Louie had arrived at our house while we were gone. We were always glad to see them. Anna Roe was still there. Uncle Gilbert was being transferred to Louisiana, and they would stay until Saturday. Sometimes they stayed for weeks when he was between construction jobs.

On June 23rd, Wil had received my letter telling him I had sent for info about the Nurses' Corps. He said he had been up since 5:30 a.m. and it was 9:30 p.m. and he still had to work some navigation problems, but I quote:

"….there is something I want straightened out. In case, you don't know what I am talking about I'll tell you. You are not going to join any Nurses' Corps or anything else. I have worked 12 months in the d,,,,,,,Navy so we could be together sometimes. I thought all along that the feeling was mutual, but I must have been wrong. If you are dissatisfied with Pulaski, I am perfectly willing for you to go anywhere else and work but I am not willing for you to go into something that will keep us from being together if we have the chance. The odds against us are high enough as it is without your making them any worse. I know you will probably think I am being unfair but if you will just recall last June you gave me the same lecture when I joined and you said that was the reason you wouldn't marry me. If this past year hasn't meant any more to you than it seems to have, then we will just drop the whole thing. The whole idea is so silly that I can't express my opinion of it. You have had some silly ideas since I have known you but this one is tops. Well that's enough of that. This is just the way I feel about it. If you still think that is what you want then don't let me stand in your way, ever."

WHEW! I don't think I ever mentioned the Nurses Corps again.

On June 24th, I wrote Wil that Roberta was spending the night, and we went (after church) up the street to James Jackson's and listened to a band he and others from the

Shoe Factory had formed We had lots of fun, and Roberta and I planned to have them at our house next Tuesday. On the night of the 24th, we all had supper at Aunt Julia'a and then went to church. Corinne and Shannon (Uncle Glbert's daughter and husband) came to spend Friday night and leave for Louisiana on Saturday.

My letter of June 25th was written after receiving his letter regarding the Nurses' Corps. I was full of apologies and reaffirmation that being with him was all I wanted or thought of. But after he told me he would choose Fighter planes and would probably go straight to the Pacific, I understood that there was no way I could be with him. I told him:

"As for my silly ideas, I don't see how you put up with me as much as you do. I realize I have very silly ideas but you knew before you loved me that I was a scatterbrain, now didn't you?"

The best way to win an argument with Wil was to agree with him.

We got up early Saturday morning after sitting up until 1 a.m., but we had to get Uncle Gilbert and family off bright and early. Paula was still visiting with Anna Roe in Elkmont so the house was quiet and lonely. On Sunday, it rained all day, and I wrote I was so lonely. Paula was coming home that afternoon, and I was glad because, *"I missed the little stink.'*

On Monday, the 28th, it was still raining and cool which was welcome. I told Wil Joyce and her new husband were at church last night, and they were a cute couple. But he didn't look to be over seventeen years old. Also I wrote that Jimmy was flying now and loved it. He sent us a navigation problem that he made a 96 on, but it was all Greek to us. Wil was getting the same training in navigation. I was going to have to work late that night because they were getting ready to send out a shipment of Army boots. We would ship about 10,000 pairs at a time, and each pair had a number. I had to type each number on the shipping order, so it was tedious and stressful. I had to be accurate.

On the night of June 29th, Roberta and I had the band from General Shoe come to our house, and we had a nice time singing and listening to them play I wrote Wil a hurried letter on Wednesday morning. I had gotten up early to write but said I had to hurry and fix Roberta some breakfast so we could get to work.

A letter from Wil written June 30th was apologizing for not writing more often, but he said they were so busy he had not had an hour to do anything in two weeks. He was upset in that letter because he was being sent to the outlying field again for just one more hour of flying. He had finished instrument flying on Saturday, and since he was in the first 25 to finish he had to take radio classes.   That was going to throw him behind about two weeks, and he didn't know why everything had to happen to him. He had been accepted in the Marines and they had ordered his uniforms. He had had his final exam in celestial navigation. He said it was hard, and he was glad it was over. He sent me an article about Torpedo Bombers.

And so June of 1943 became history.

39 BEGINNING OF JULY 1943

July 1943: I began the month of July by getting up at 5:30 a.m. to write to Wil. I felt so well that morning that I told him I felt I could turn the world over.
I had just been feeling so tired and run down that a good morning was a pleasant surprise. We had heard from Jimmy, and he had taken a ten hour exam intended to flunk out about half of them. He wasn't sure he had passed but we got a Special Delivery letter the next day saying he had passed ok.

I wrote again that night after getting the letter from Wil written on June 30th in which he was so disgusted with things at Pensacola. I told him it had been cool the last two days, so it made me feel better. I wrote him a pep letter pointing out that he had come too far to drop out now. He was like me, just had some days when he felt like throwing in the towel. The War was beginning to drag everyone down. Daddy and Nancye had gone fishing that afternoon, and as soon as they came in, we were all going to a show. Pulaski closed all their businesses on Thursday afternoon, except the factories.

On July 2nd, we were still having some unseasonably cool weather that was certainly welcome. On that day, Daddy finally completed his little farm in town. He bought a cow. Now we had a cow, chickens, rabbits and a garden.

Poor Daddy never really got to be a big farmer but after the War he did get his thirteen acres. Mama was so happy to have the cow. She named her Bessie. I wrote Nancye was thrilled to death because Mama was fixing to milk the cow and Nancye had never seen that done before. Bessie was great. We had all the milk, butter and whipping cream we could use and often shared it with neighbors. That little farm in town was only four doors up the street from where I live now, seventy five years later.

July 4th was on Sunday that year, and we had a holiday on Monday. I wrote that we had all been invited to a big barbecue after church at the Crescent View Farms. The Weaver family lived there at that time, and they had seven or eight children. Lots of church people were there.

I told Wil I had to work half a day on Saturday the 3rd and then made myself a dress Saturday afternoon. I had to make a pinafore on my holiday because I was to serve Cokes at an upcoming factory party, and we had to wear pinafores.

I was wondering if Wil would get a holiday for the Fourth and what he would do. He never told me about any of his activities when he was free to leave the base. But it wasn't his nature to tell everything like it was mine. Anyway, my cousin, Laura Dew Jones, was home from college. Her cadet boyfriend was being transferred. She said it was killing her, but I told her it wouldn't kill her; she would just wish at times she was dead. He was sent overseas and was killed. She later married his best friend.

There were a lot of girls who had gotten married before their men were called, and so I knew a lot of wives who had small babies. I wanted one of my own so badly. Some of them, their fathers had never seen. I guess Wil did have the day off on the Fourth because he wrote me a four page letter.

I did not write on the 6th but got up early on the 7th to write. I kept complaining that I was so tired all the time and could not gain any weight. I had gone with Roberta the night before to help decorate the garage we were using for the factory party coming up that Friday night. I was not much help because one of the girls brought her baby, and I played with it. Wil had been in the Air Corps officially one year July 6th.

I answered his letter of the 4th and told him I didn't know myself why I didn't marry him before he left. I said I think I was afraid of too much happiness I said I didn't think I had really grown up on July 4, 1942, so I thought I was just too afraid and uncertain. But we both were glad we waited because I was just as proud of his being a pilot as he was. I told him I worried about his safety but never once felt that he would fail to make a good pilot. I felt that our being apart had strengthened our love. If he had not been faithful to me, I did not want to know it but I felt that he had and I knew I had been faithful to him.

My Daddy sold his car that week and we all cried.. It was a Chevrolet. I don't remember what year, but we felt like we had lost a member of the family. He got $525.00 for it, and he felt it was too good to turn down. Jimmy had written that there were only fourteen left in his class, but he was still in. I never doubted his ability to hang in there either. I told Wil that, yes, I cried when I got so lonesome. Sometimes it just seemed like everything was bigger than I was, and I just had to cry over it. I never told him but I was having health problems. I just felt exhausted.

I was up at 5:30 a.m. the 9th to write to him. Roberta had spent the night again, and we had worked the night before on decorating for the party that night. I was wishing I didn't have to go, but they had a problem getting girls to serve because all of them wanted to dance. Roberta and I were about the only ones who would not be dancing Daddy bought a 1940 Chevrolet that day, and it was a nicer car than he sold and he got it for only $5.00 more than the old one sold for. He put new upholstery in it, so it was pretty nice. I told Wil to remind me to spend the rest of my life telling him how much I loved him. He never had to remind me, for I told him every day.

Pulaski was very sad the weekend of July 9th. The son of one of the lawyers in town, Dick Dodson, died at sea the Monday before and word was received on Friday. I had gone to school with Dick. I told Wil he was in my French class and always copied my exam paper. He was an only child. He got his Wings five weeks prior to his death and had sailed for overseas three weeks before. I think the ship was attacked. The War was really taking a toll on our boys.

In my letter to Wil of July 10th, I wrote that when the little sisters were playing croquet, some little boy was throwing rocks. Peggy was hit in the head with one and had a big goose egg. Everything seemed to happen to her and she never bothered anyone.

On Sunday, July 11th, after church, I was so lonely I walked to Aunt Julia's to visit with her, Evelyn and Martha. Wil called while I was gone. He talked to Mama and was all right. I immediately put in a call for him, but they could not locate him, so I was really disappointed. I wrote him a letter telling him it would make no difference to me if he got washed out. I was going to love him forever anyway. Communication was so poor during the War. Letters were about it. It was so hard to get a phone call through. Sometimes we sent telegrams if it was an urgent matter. But no one liked to see the Western Union delivery man coming up the walk because it could have been bad news from the War Department like the Dodsons received.

He called me again on Monday night, the 12th. I told him in a letter I wrote immediately after hanging up that talking to him made me want to see him so bad I could scream. I was so blue and unhappy. Paula and I were there alone. Mama, Daddy and the other two girls had gone to Uncle Buster's. And it was raining. But I was mostly upset because I wanted to see him so badly. I asked him:

"Does it ever occur to you that our conversations are always so one sided? I get tired of doing all the talking, believe it or not. I wanted to hear you tell me something that I could think about and instead all I heard from you was Yes and No."

He was really the silent type, and I was a chatterbox. But we suited each other.

40 END OF JULY 1943

I had called his folks and talked to his Dad to see when they were planning to go to Pensacola, but they had decided they could not go. So Daddy said we would all go the next Sunday and see the Cordells. Paula and her friend, Mary Beth, rode the train to Nashville on Thursday, the 15th, and we went up on the Sunday. The girls went to visit with Pansy for the two or three days, and we brought them back. Mother Cordell had as much company as my Mother did, but families really enjoyed being together back then. The Sunday we went up there, all of the Cordell family came except for Lawrence, Myrtle and their children. Dad Cordell got off from work at noon and he and Daddy talked all afternoon "as hard as they could".

Wil called to talk to all of us that day, and I told him Dad Cordell was just like a little kid when he called. And so was I. Wil really made an effort to talk to me that time, and I really felt good after that call. Everyone had a new baby, it seemed, but me. And I wanted one so bad. I told Wil his cousin, Robert Lawrence, had the cutest baby, and I got to hold him. Of course, Wayne and Bobbi Jean and Denny were there. It was just a wonderful Sunday for all of us, and my family felt so elegant in the "new" car with the new upholstery. When the War started, most of us were just crawling out of the Depression Years, and the War brought more prosperity as well as sadness and loneliness.

We still had not gotten a raise at the Shoe Factory,, and now that they were withholding tax from our pay, I felt it really was not worth working in such a hot, dirty place,. I was really thinking about handing in my notice, so I would be sure to not be working if Wil got his furlough.

No matter how often I heard from Wil, it was never enough. But I didn't dare miss a day writing to him. Looking back I can see I followed the same pattern in writing to him as I did in talking. Even if he didn't answer, I had to keep feeding him information.

I still remember how hot the month of July was and how tired I felt all of the time. Roberta and I had been coming home to Mama for lunch every day, but we had to start packing our lunch because it was just too hot to walk home and back at noon time. Mama said it made the day too long when we didn't come. Of course, the little girls were always there.

Wil wrote me on Wednesday night, the 21st:

"….since I haven't written you this week, I thought you might be getting a little mad by now".

He loved to push my buttons! He told me I owed him $2.65 for the call he made Sunday. He said I could keep it, and he would collect it in kisses when he saw me. He asked:

"About how many will I get?"

He had had a rough day. First, he was put on report for being absent from bunk check. He said he wasn't absent, so he wouldn't sign the report. That made the officer mad, and he said that he would see that Wil signed it. But, he still hadn't signed it, and he would quit the corps before he would sign it. He could really be stubborn when he thought he was right but I guess he got by with not signing. On top of that he had gotten a 1.0 in aptitude because he was the leader in flying. Since they held the leader responsible for everything that happened, Wil got the 1.0. You were only allowed to get two of them before getting kicked out. He said he got more disgusted with the Navy every day. But he did not want to give up flying He said it wasn't much of a letter; he wasn't blue, just disgusted. He ended with:

"Anyway, I love you so what else matters?"

I also wrote him on the 21st, of course, and told him he would not only be getting a good cook and housekeeper but a musician as well because Daddy bought a player piano that day. It was second hand but a nice one, and I immediately started to bang on it when I got home. Daddy could chord on it pretty well. All of my life, I had longed to play a musical instrument, so they had to drag me away from it to go to Prayer Meeting. Like my love for dolls and seeing that I got them, Wil never forgot my yearning to play music. So as soon as he felt that we were able to afford it, about fifteen years after we married, he gave me my first organ, and I took lessons.

My answer to his letter about owing him for the phone call, I said:

"Darling, it was worth $10.00 to be able to talk to you last Sunday. But please don't start rating my loving in terms of money because you would be in debt to me for the rest of your life".

I told him a new couple had moved in two doors from us. They had a new baby, so I was already looking forward to holding it. I had bought it a little silver spoon and was going up to see the baby that afternoon. The only thing Wil was never able to give me that I really wanted was several children. That was my fault, not his. We had planned on a large family.

On Sunday, the 25th, I told him I had dreaded that day after such a wonderful time with his family the last Sunday. It was Jimmy's birthday, and he was alone in California. The Fox family children and several others from church came and we had a watermelon feast so the day was a nice one. I told him I still missed him even in a crowd, but that I had rather have him to myself than in a crowd because he was always sweeter when we were alone. In a crowd, he always looked like he was afraid someone would think he did care for me. I wrote:

"That is one thing I have never understood but I never have bothered to question the things I don't understand about you, Darling, because I just kind of like you any old way."

Jimmy was getting quite a bit of flying by this time.. They were going to make a 10-hour bomber flight up to Salt Lake City the next day (16th). He had already made two short trips. So now we had to worry about his being in the air also. For his birthday, I had sent him stationery and stamps, and Daddy sent him a money belt.

My hair was long, and the weather was so hot, but Wil never wanted my hair cut. I did get a permanent, and that made it draw up a little, but I assured him it would be grown out by the time he got his furlough. I was wishing he could find out when he might be home as I was really feeling I needed to do something about my job. I wanted him to tell me what he thought I should do about quitting. I wanted assurances that he could not give me as to whether I would be able to go with him when he left Pensacola. I was telling him about the disgraceful things going on at the factory. Married men were going with single girls and vice -versa. It had gotten so bad, I said, I was afraid of being talked about myself, so much gossip.

But I conducted myself the way I had been raised and if I was ever talked about it did not reach my ears. I was really a very naive, innocent nineteen year old and Wil liked it that way.

41 BAGS OF BONES

On July 26th, Wil got six letters from me. Finally they
had all caught up with him. He had started firing machine
guns that day. They would have two weeks of that on the
ground and about three weeks of it in the air. He liked it fine,
but thought it was going to be pretty tough. They were really
turning my guy into a tough Marine fighting machine.

The War in Europe was looking better for the Allies.
There was a movement in Italy to depose Mussolini because
the Italians were weary of military disasters, and they knew
that mainland Italy would soon be conquered by the Allies.
But Mussolini was close to Hitler, and he refused to tell Hitler
that Italy wished to surrender. The Fascist Guard Council
realized they could no longer depend on Mussolini's
leadership so the Council decided to bring back the King to
lead the demoralized armed forces, King Victor Emmanuel
III was willing to come out of obscurity and resume Italy's
leadership. But Mussolini could not be persuaded to resign.
On Sunday, July 25th, Mussolini went to see the King who
was surrounded by Italian "carabinieri" (Italian Police), and
Mussolini, now ex-dictator was taken into protective custody
and was spirited away in an ambulance. Within 48 hours, he
was interred on the island of Ponaz thus ending his 21 years
of one-man-rule of Italy. Regardless of that good news the
War would grind on for two more years.

On July 26th, I wrote that the factory was almost

unbearable. I loved the people, but the noise and the heat were awful. On the 27th, I had a funny spell at work and had another one that night. So on the 28th, I wrote a short note telling Wil not to worry but I was having a day or two of rest due to what the doctor called nervous exhaustion. My heart was what scared us. I have had a heart murmur from a faulty mitral valve all of my life, and the doctor said I had a very rapid heartbeat, but it could be just from nerves. He said the noise at the factory was enough to kill anyone, so he immediately asked if I would consider the bookkeeper's job at the hospital because the girl they had was not satisfactory. He put me on iron tonic and I hoped to go back to work in a few days. I had sent Wil a cake by mail. I hoped it wasn't melted.

August 1943 was a very stressful month for all of us. The spells I had were more debilitating than I had thought they would be. I tried to go back to work but just couldn't hold out. I told my boss to just find someone else. He said for me to rest a few days and see if I could come back. Meanwhile Pansy was pretty sick, and we were not sure what was wrong with her. Mother Cordell wanted me to come to Nashville and keep Pansy company, but I felt I had to get back to work as soon as I could. Then my doctor intervened and told them I would have to be off from work at least a month. So I drew some sick pay, and Mama made me stay in bed. She would fuss when she caught me up trying to write to Wil.

I did not hear from him as he was having it rough also. It was their final month of intense training, practice battles and night flying, but I wanted to hear so badly that I began to fuss at him for not writing

I remember how wonderful everyone was to me while I was sick. I wrote Wil that people had sent me ice cream, cherry cokes, malted milks, etc., and one of the neighbors brought a big piece of cherry pie with whipped cream on it while I was writing to him Mama told me to tell Wil I was so thin everyone felt sorry for me. I was worried how Wil would feel about my being just a bag of bones.

News from Jimmy was good. He was really happy

getting to fly. He had 36 hours in the air by that time. He seemed more thrilled with flying than Wil did, if possible. He wasn't the pilot, of course, but they were still in danger. They almost hit a high-tension wire one day so that news worried us.

I finally got a letter from Wil on August 4th. I had told Wil I had been so sick I didn't care if lived or died, but I was feeling better. News from Nashville was that Pansy was better. Wil's letter was telling me how much weight he had lost. I kept bugging him to tell me when he thought he would graduate, if he could get home and could we get married? He had stopped mentioning anything about it anymore. I ended the letter I wrote on the 4th that Pansy had called and was better and she was planning to come and visit the next week.

My letter of August 7th, I was feeling better and had baked a cake that day. I told him Aunt Julia wanted me to bake one for her to send to her son, Howard, in the service, I was a good cook and a good seamstress then but am a failure at both now.

The week of August 8th, the wife of Bro. Elmer Smith, who was our preacher for several years, came for a visit. She brought her baby daughter, and they stayed a week. I really enjoyed them, especially the baby. Also, Nancye's little friend, Beverly Berry, was staying with us because her Mother was in the hospital. I wrote that the little girls were having a grand time but I didn't know what we would do with two like them all the time.

Wil had written me that if I went to Nashville he would give me permission to date one of Pansy's boyfriends. I told him I hoped he was kidding because I did not want him dating anyone else. I felt if we dated anyone else, we no longer cared for each other. I said:

"At least I feel like that's the way it would be for me. But, anyhow, I don't worry much about that because you promised to tell me if you ever tired of me. I know you well enough to know you'll keep a promise. That's one thing I believe, that you are truthful and I am proud of it."

I told him Daddy was going to let me drive the new car the next day (Sunday). And I guess he did but I was not a good driver at all back then.

Mary W. Cordell

42 AUGUST 1943

I got word from Pansy that she was still having the painful attacks and she was afraid to come down here. So I made plans to go up there the next Thursday or Friday. I told Wil I was going to stay up there until I wanted to come home, but I would probably want to see Mama by Sunday. The factory had gone ahead and hired a new girl, but I wrote Wil that a lawyer in town asked me to work as his bookkeeper and the hospital still wanted me as soon as I was able to work. I wrote Wil that something was telling me I would never work again in public work. Boy, was I wrong!! I wrote also that I felt so silly that night I could talk the horns off a billy goat. I asked:

"How will you ever put up with me? Did you ever get tired of me talking. It used to be so funny how I would rattle off and you would never say a word and I always had the feeling that what I said went in one ear and out the other, but I was glad because what I said didn't amount to a hill of beans anyway. I'm afraid that if you called me tonight I would run up a $20.00 phone bill, which reminds me, did the cake make up for the $2.65 worth of kisses I owe you? Because you know kissing does spread diseases and I so want to be a lady, a real one, for once. Just to show you that I can 'cause -well you know. Well, you have to forget a few things when you love someone so much and you see them

188

once in a blue moon and I do so hope you know it was
because I love you so much and not because I am bad.
Anyone reading this might think I had committed a crime if
they didn't know what I was talking about."

But he knew that I really worried that I let him kiss me.
By today's standards I was about three years old.

The week of August 10th Mrs. Smith and her baby were
there. Mrs. Smith let me drive her car some that week so I
could get used to the gear shift on the steering wheel. It was
still in the floor on most cars. I was still planning to go to
Nashville on Thursday. Mama wanted to be sure I was
strong enough to go. I wrote that Charlie Tucker and Bob
Abernathy, two local boys, were on furlough and had come
to see me. They were ready to go overseas.

So I went to Nashville. Got a ride with someone but I
forget who. Pansy had gotten worse and was in the hospital
by the time I got there. She had a stone in her appendix, but
she made it fine through the surgery. They all insisted that I
stay, so I would be there when she came home. So I did.
The house was so quiet and peaceful after all the traffic and
activities at our house. I was getting some much needed
rest. I got there on Wednesday, the 11th. My ride had let
me out at the 7th Avenue Garage and I took a taxi to the
Cordell residence. I told Wil I had a nice chat with the taxi
driver and that no one was at the Cordell's but Susie, a black
lady who helped Mother Cordell. I told him Susie had told me
all about her boyfriend, so I had been well entertained. Also
Robert Lawrence and his little family had an apartment
upstairs so I could go up there and play with their baby. I
was afraid I would be an extra burden on Mother Cordell, but
she and Dad Cordell assured me they wanted me to stay
and be with Pansy. I was not an invalid, so I helped all I
could. I went to the hospital one or two days, so Mother
Cordell could stay at home. I wrote Wil that Pansy and I
laughed so much I was afraid she would tear her stitches. I
just loved being with Wil's family.

A letter from Wil on August 9th and forwarded to me in
Nashville had good news and bad. He wrote he had a bad

day. They didn't get to fly because of a mix-up in schedules. Then he went to town to get his laundry, and it wasn't back. He said it had been six weeks, so he had cursed everyone out. To top it all off, a good friend was killed while flying that day. He said that made six friends he had lost since he had been In Pensacola. But good news was that they were winding down, and he was pretty sure he would get four or five days of travel time.

After he found out I was in Nashville, he wanted me to stay there until he came home because he wanted to see me first, but it would be nice to see all of us at the same time. I told him I wanted to do that, but Mama thought I should come home and then go back to Nashville before Wil got there. He didn't like it because I was trying to do what Mama thought I should instead of what he wanted I always tried to do what both of them wanted so I was torn between the two. After a few heated letters were exchanged, I did what Wil asked and stayed there.

While I was there, Clifford and Elizabeth's house burned to the ground. So they all came to Mother Cordell's. Shirley was a baby then, and there were Wayne and Bobbi. No one was hurt and they saved all of their furniture. I had the job of telling Wil about that because his mother said he had to know and he might hear it from someone else. I told him I didn't think I had ever loved his Mother as much as I did the night of the fire I said she is so wonderful about taking her troubles. She was such a strong, sweet Christian woman.

I wrote that a long letter from John Alton let everyone know he was all right wherever he was.

On the 6th, I wrote that Elizabeth took Wayne and went to Detroit to visit her mother. Auntie and Uncle Horace took Bobbi Jean and Myrtle and Lawrence kept Shirley. I had gone to a family reunion with Thomas and Sarah Hamlett and enjoyed their little boy who was two months old. Thomas had been deferred from the service until November. He had stayed out of the War longer than any of Wil's other buddies.

Mama was still pressuring me to come home, but I felt she wanted to try to talk me out of getting married until after the War. I was determined not to be persuaded. I was still writing Wil and wondering why he was not talking (writing) about it anymore. He told me later that he had the plans made but didn't want to tell me anything because I had been disappointed so many times before and he could not tell me anything for certain. I did go ahead and plan on it though. Daddy said they would come to Nashville so that we could have the car. He was always on my side in anything I wanted.

Wil was so sure he would be sent overseas after he graduated that he was pretending that was just what he wanted. I told him it hurt me for him to want to go because that made it seem he had nothing to stay in the States for. Those were happy and unhappy days. The suspense was killing me.

Pansy was recuperating nicely and back home after about eight or nine days. She and I had so much fun together. I loved being with all of them.

After getting the letter from Wil telling me about cursing out the laundry people, I wrote him a pretty firm letter about losing his temper. I had meant to try to talk to him about that before we married but was afraid we would not have any time to talk. And I wanted him to know I expected him to respect me and not yell at me when I did something he didn't like. I was just upset because he had not reassured me of his love lately. He wrote the nicest letter when he received mine. That made me sorry I had said anything. He told me:

"I don't think there has ever been a time that I wanted to hurt you. Maybe I have said things that hurt you but that wasn't the reason I said them. I think our whole trouble is that somewhere deep down in your heart you aren't exactly sure that I love you. That isn't your fault. I love you more than anything or anybody I know of. Since I know it and haven't the slightest doubt about it, it never seemed to occur to me that you couldn't be sure of it unless I did more than tell you every 4 or 5 weeks. You told me you loved me. I accepted it and it made me very happy, but you continued to

tell me and you did your best to prove it. Mary, the first time you told me that you loved me, I think that was the happiest moment I have known, even though both of us knew that you weren't sure. You were the first girl that I ever wanted to love enough to marry. I know it is hard for you to believe this for I never write a decent letter to you unless I get one from you like I got today. Mary, that is one reason I am doubtful about marrying you. If I hurt you now there is no telling what would happen if we married. As for getting married that is one thing I have tried my best to spare your feelings on. I don't want you to be disappointed so therefore haven't given you anything definite. I know that if I were to tell you anything that would give you the least bit of hope that you would make plans just as I have already done. So don't worry about it for I have planned what to do no matter what my orders say. Maybe you feel that I should tell you so you could share them, but there are too many chances of things being changed. I won't know exactly what will happen until one hour after I am designated and receive my orders. So please try to understand that I do love you more than you know and haven't the least desire to hurt you. I am sorry for hurting you so let's drop it and no more crying, huh? Goodnight, Darling – Yours, Wilburn"

That letter made my day and I made up my mind not to doubt him again.

43 A WEDDING!

I received one more letter from him saying he would be home August 28th and to tell his Mother to make his cake a wedding cake. I had written him a sweet letter and he said after reading it he felt that he had finally achieved success. He had made his last hop, and he got my love letter telling him again I wanted to marry him. He didn't know which made him happier.

So the long wait was coming to an end. My Daddy sent money and Mother Cordell took me shopping for a wedding dress. I bought a blue crepe dress, shoes and purse to match and gown and robe. Mother Cordell organized the reception in their back yard. My parents came up on Saturday morning, August 28th. Just about the time they arrived we got a call from Wil's buddy, Gerald Green who lived in Nashville and had trained with Wil all along. He informed us that due to some mix up of Wil's papers, he had been delayed the night before and would probably be unable to catch his train so that he could be home by Saturday night. So, as usual, I cried. My wedding day was going to be all messed up and we had worked so hard that week to be ready. We really did not know what to do as we had invited several people as well as the Cordell and Lawrence families to attend the Reception. We had also contacted a preacher we knew in Franklin, Kentucky to be ready to marry us that afternoon. There was a waiting period of three days in Tennessee and Wil only had four days leave, so we had to go to Kentucky to be married. No waiting period there. But that was a very disconcerting Saturday morning.

Dad Cordell had gone to work that morning at Union Station where he went every day but Sunday. The rest of us were just sitting around wondering what we should do. The phone rang and I answered it, hoping it was Wil.

It was Dad Cordell and he said, "Mary, Wilburn is here at the station". He had made it after all and I never knew how he accomplished it. Daddy, Pansy and I jumped in the car to go to the station to pick them up. Excitement was on again. Wil looked so good in his officer's uniform and I thought he was the handsomest man I had ever seen. He took me to be alone for a few minutes and he really wanted to be sure I knew what I was doing and that it was what I wanted. I convinced him that I never wanted anything so badly in my life before.

Daddy, Clifford, Evelyn and Pansy went with us to Franklin and we went to the Courthouse and got the license. Then we went to Bro. Adamson's home where he and his wife had decorated their living room with beautiful flowers and had an altar set up. Clifford was Best Man and Pansy was my Maid of Honor.

And so I was finally married to the man I loved. I was so happy, so tired, and so exhausted, that I hardly knew what was going on, but we made it back to Nashville to be ready for the Reception.

Dad Cordell had been on the phone all day trying to find a hotel room for us but there were no vacancies. There were no motels fit to sleep in those days, so Wil and I had no choice but to accept Auntie and Uncle Horace's invitation to spend our wedding night in their front bedroom.

It was after 10 p.m. before the party broke up and we all had to scatter to find the places where we would sleep. It was almost midnight by the time Wil and I got ready to settle down for the night. And I was almost to the point of exhaustion, both happy and scared to death. Nothing had prepared me for the first night; no one had talked to me about it, what was expected of me or how to hide my shyness and ignorance. I hid in the closet to undress and came out in my new dimity gown and housecoat. I owned no house shoes Wil was already in bed in his red and white striped pajamas. He just grinned and watched me while I made the final step to join him.

I never loved Wil Cordell more than I did that night. When I crawled in bed, he gathered me to him and gave me a big, long kiss. Then he turned me over and cuddled up spoon style and told me:

"You are so tired. I want you to go to sleep now and feel better tomorrow."

So I did, content for the first time in months. I wrote him much later when he was overseas fighting that I wondered what he thought about my hiding in the closet to undress. He wrote back, *"If you hadn't, I would have."* We were both so innocent and so in love.

He had four days and we spent it with family, either in Nashville or Pulaski. Mama, Daddy, Pansy, the girls, and I took him to Birmingham the night of September 1st where he got on a train headed to Jacksonville, Florida, and we did not know where else at that time.

So I was now a married woman and still without my sweetheart. I started writing letters that night and had to hold them until I received his first letter, giving me an address. I mailed him five or six letters as soon as I heard and I tried to settle down to wait for him. So many of my friends were in the same boat, married and waiting for the War to end, so we could begin our lives. I had thought it would be easier if we were married but it wasn't. Wil did not want me to go back to work, yet there was nothing to take my mind off of him and wondering if he would come back to me all right or would he be sent overseas right away. But he wrote every chance he had and did all he could to encourage me. He said he felt better over things than he had in some time but he wished we could be together. I was making plans and after two weeks, I decided I was going to be with him even if it was only for a few days if it was possible at all.

I wrote him after two weeks and told him I was coming to Jacksonville unless he told me I couldn't. But he called me as soon as he heard and he was delighted. He had been afraid that I was not able to leave Pulaski yet, and also he still had no idea what they would do with them now that they were through training. But we took our chances and I rode the bus to Jacksonville. I had to stand up all the way to Chattanooga, made a change there and found a seat. We changed buses again in Atlanta and I was able to get a seat. The trains and buses were always full of service men trying to get to where they had to be and no one made allowances for civilians who dared to travel during those rugged and hurtful times. So I did not encounter very many women on that trip and it took about fourteen hours of travel time.

And so my life with my husband was beginning and I was so excited I forgot to be frightened by what I was doing. I know now that God was looking after me or I would never have made it.

44 JACKSONVILLE ADVENTURE

When I embarked from the bus at about 1 p.m. the next day, I felt as if I had landed on the moon. Things were so strange to me. Compared to my small town of Pulaski, Jacksonville seemed to be wall-to-wall people, automobiles, street cars, and buildings after buildings. I had no idea where to go first. I collected my luggage, which consisted of one fully packed suitcase, which held almost all of the clothes I owned, a make-up kit with a shoulder strap and my purse. My suitcase was so heavy I could hardly lift it but I did and I left the bus station carrying it. But I had no idea which direction to go so I just started walking toward what looked like the center of the city. I stopped one or two people to ask the way to the hotel Wil had told me to go to but no one seemed to have the time to do more than just point me in the right direction. So I just kept walking. Such a green horn that I never thought of getting a taxi. Finally I spotted my destination and when I reached it, I was almost ready to faint from the heat and the need of something to eat and drink.

I went to the hotel clerk at the desk and told him my name. It felt strange to say I was Mrs. Cordell. He slid the Register book around for me to sign but I had carried the heavy suitcase so long that my fingers would not uncurl so I could hold the pen. It was against rules to let a woman alone go to a room without signing in. The clerk took pity on me and told me to go with the busboy and he would take me to my room. He said to rest and come back down later and sign in. I had just met my first angel unaware in this journey I had embarked on. I did as he said, rested, had a bath and clean clothes. Then I went back and signed in. I went back to the room to wait for Wil for I was afraid to wander out into the crowded streets alone. Frankly I was scared to death, I already missed Mama and Daddy and the little girls but I was excited also as I waited for my husband to come through the door.

It was a joyous reunion as I think Wil had really been surprised at my decision to join him regardless of what little time we might have. He was as excited as I was. He looked so good in his uniform and I wondered again how I had ever attracted such a handsome man. We went to the hotel restaurant for supper and then back to our room to catch up with each other and make plans. That day was Friday and Wil had the week end off so my trip was going to be worth it.

On Saturday, we set out to find a place for me to live while there as we could not afford the hotel for over two nights. We perused the want ads for advertisements and finally found a nice bedroom on Herschel Street, with two elderly people who were trying to supplement their income as well as help out with housing the many service people who had come there. The bedroom was very nice with a side door that opened onto a side porch with a swing and a couple of rockers. We did not have kitchen privileges but there were places to eat nearby where I could walk when I wanted to eat. I ate very little anyway. But I settled in to do my best to enjoy being with my sweet Wil for as long as time permitted. He would slip off the base every night and come to be with me and leave early in the morning to slip back on the base. I guess he would have been court-martialed if they had caught him. I was very happy and so glad I had made the trip.

I settled in as it looked as if they would be in Jacksonville for two or three months to get training over the ocean. I found that I could easily walk to the main part of downtown so I volunteered to do something to help the war effort. They had a huge map of Jacksonville and surrounding territory on

a huge sunken floor and it was populated with small
airplanes and ships and surrounded with a wrought iron
fence which kept us from falling overboard. We were
furnished with long slender poles with a magnet on the end,
and the ships and planes had magnets. We wore ear pieces
and had to listen intently to the voice that was constantly
talking. When a plane or ship appeared close to
Jacksonville we were instructed to assign one of the little
planes to the tip of our pole and we were told just where to
push it around on the map. This was the same for any ships
which approached the harbor. That way, we were aware at
all times if any foreign traffic was coming our way and it was
tracked until we were told to release it. That took up quite a
bit of my time. I met other people there, but no one in the
same situation as I was, so we did not become close friends.

There were several movies in the area so I could always
spend a couple of hours alone in one of them waiting until
Wil could get in to go eat supper with me. I read a lot as I
loved books so I managed to fill my time. It was the first time
in my life that I had nothing that was demanded or necessary
that I take care of so it was like a whole new life. And it was
anyway – I now belonged to the man I loved more than I
loved myself.

I stayed in close touch with my family and Wil's by letter
and maybe one or two phone calls every month. And time
seemed to fly by. Then things changed again. I knew when
Wil came in for that weekend that something was worrying
him but he would not confide in me until late Sunday before
he had to leave for the base. I was going to have to go
home. They were to start night flying the next night and he
would not be able to slip into town to be with me and he was
not willing for me to be in the big city alone. We had
managed to save $85.00 in a small bank account in
Jacksonville. I always managed to have a little money put
back and Wil did also, so we felt rich with that $85.00. He
told me that he would leave me enough cash to get a taxi to
the bus station the next day and I could go to the bank and
close out our account which would give me bus money as
well as something to eat on and enough to run on until my

allotment was started, which was already in the works.

And so he left me early that Monday morning and I pushed all my belongings back into the big suitcase and make-up kit, took up my purse, and bade farewell to the older couple who had been so nice to us. I paid the taxi driver and had about fifty cents left after I ate a little breakfast. I checked my bags, along with a small, battery-operated portable radio Wil had given me, into a drawer at the bus station, stashed the key in my purse and set out for the bank. I was familiar with the city by now and knew where to go but as I walked up the streets I noticed a lack of traffic, no pedestrians as usual and the whole city seemed to be on lock down. When I reached the bank, a sign on the door said: CLOSED FOR VETERAN'S DAY. In our anxiety over being parted again, neither of us had remembered the holiday. Now what was I to do? I knew no one in Jacksonville well enough to ask them for help. I had no money to buy food for the day, or to rent a hotel room, and had no choice but to spend the night in a filthy, hot bus station surrounded by service men from every part of the country, and I probably would not find a place to sit down. So as was my usual way of facing things, I cried as I walked back toward the bus station. And I asked God for help every step I took.

I had to pause at a red light and I looked down the street to my left and saw one little dress shop that looked as if it was open. I hurried down there and it was open for business. I looked around and picked out a brown crepe dress and shoes to match and a pink felt skirt with a black poodle on it, very popular at the time. My purchases came to $12.00. I timidly asked if I could make my check for $25.00 which would give me $13.00 to get my ticket and a little food. The clerk said, "Oh, no, I cannot do that", so I burst out crying She ran and got the manager and I calmed down enough to tell him my predicament. That unaware angel said, "I am going to cash your check." I thanked him profusely and I thanked God, took my new clothes and $13.00 and purse and hurried back toward the bus station. It was almost time for my bus to load and so I grabbed my belongings from the locker, hurried to buy my ticket and dragged everything to the loading dock.

Again I was dismayed at the crowd of people already lined up to board the bus to Birmingham. I had to go to the end of the line so I started begging God again. "Oh, God. I still may have to spend the night in the station. Lord, I am so scared. Please help me get on this bus". I am sure I made a lot of promises of how good I would be if He would help me. But it looked so hopeless.

The bus driver opened the door and stepped down. He announced, "Service Men first." And sailors, soldiers and Marines scrambled to get on. Buses were much smaller then than now. It looked as if it was full by that time and still a long line waiting ahead of me. The driver announced again, "All those travelling with Service men load next." and people started scrambling on board again. I knew then that my luck had run out so I started to gather up my load to go back inside when I heard the driver say, "You back there, hurry up and get on board," I looked to see who he was talking to and he was pointing at me and waving me to hurry. So I hurried. He grabbed my bag and threw it under the bus into the luggage carrier and I hastened to climb into the bus as quickly as I could.

Once in there I did not know where I was supposed to sit as the Service men were busy getting their wives and traveling partners seated. I had no idea what to do until I spotted a soldier close the back of the bus. He was standing by two seats. He placed his finger over his lips and motioned for me to come back there which I did without question. When I reached him he took my package, make-up kit and radio and stored them overhead. He sat down and whispered, "Don't say anything. I told him you are my wife." Suddenly that soldier sprouted wings that he was unaware of having. He was such a gentleman. He said I looked as if I had lost my last friend. I told him I had not known what I was going to do.

We talked and dozed until we arrived in Birmingham after dark and he stayed with me until I was safely on the bus to Pulaski. I thought I would never forget the names of the two men who had helped me that day but I have forgotten. But I will never forget the two unaware angels God sent to help me that very scary day. I really think there was a third angel unaware that day. I really do not think that the bus driver believed that I was that soldier's wife, but he let me on the bus anyway.

Now if there is any moral to this story it is this. If you are ever in a strange place, alone with no money, hungry and no place to stay when night comes, and you wish you had someone to talk to who would listen, just do as I did, and talk to GOD

45 MIAMI

I hardly slept at all on the bus that night, thinking of the distressing day I had had and of the lovely people who helped me. My Daddy was waiting for me at the bus station at 4 a.m. that morning and I cried as I hugged him. I was so happy to be back home safely and yet so upset that I had been torn away from Wil again with no say so in it at all and nothing he could do either.

Mama was up and had breakfast on the way when we arrived home and the girls were up and excited that I was back. My room was still waiting for me and Mama made me rest some that morning. Then the rest of the day, we spent talking about what had happened in Pulaski while I was away and they all wanted to hear about my stay in Jacksonville. So I settled in again to wait for the War to end so we could get on with our lives.

I did not hear from Wil. I did send him a telegram that I had made the trip safely and I began writing every day and could mail them to him as he now had a base address where he could get mail. But I could not understand his not trying to get in touch with me some way and after a week of worrying and being aggravated, I decided that something had happened to him in night flying and he had been hurt. I tried to reach him through the base but was told that they could not give out any information on Lt. Cordell and that I should hear from him soon.

I realized that if anything was wrong, his parents would be notified first as I had not been put on the roster as being married to him. So I got on another bus and went to Nashville in order to be with the Cordells if they received any bad news. But after being up there another week, we were all getting desperate to hear something. It was very nerve wracking. And then one afternoon a taxi stopped in front of the house. I looked out to see who it was and Wil was getting out of the cab. I alerted the others in the house and ran to him, tears of joy running down my face. (I even cried when I was happy).

When everyone had settled down, Wil began to tell us what had happened. He had a very good friend who had been in training with him for several months. He was a full-blooded Indian from a reservation in Oklahoma. His name was Truman Dykes and we all called him Chief. I had been with him quite a bit with Wil while in Jacksonville. On the first night of night flying, while I was traveling all night to Tennessee, they were flying in formation. Wil was the Squadron leader and Chief was flying closely to his right side when all of a sudden his plane started going down. Wil had to watch, not knowing what was happening until he saw it hit the ground and burst into flames. Will led the other planes back to the base and reported the accident. Chief was burned up in the plane and it took two or three days to get his body in any shape to put into a casket and seal it completely tight. Wil was designated to take the body to Oklahoma and have a military funeral. He was to guard the casket night and day and was told he would be court-martialed if the casket was opened for any reason. They did not want the family or the public to see what could happen to our boys here in America let alone after they went overseas. Wil was under orders to tell no one where he was going or why and they could not divulge any information from the base. Over two weeks had passed before Wil had performed all of his duties regarding the funeral and dealing with the Dykes family. He was given permission to come back through Nashville and have four days rest before reporting back to Jacksonville. He was so elated that I was in

Nashville so he could see all of us together. After two nights with his folks, we both went to Pulaski and had one night there. The next day, we had to take him once again to Birmingham to get a train to Florida but that time, we decided that I would travel back with him and see what happened. And so my suitcase was packed again and we spent a wonderful night traveling on the train in a cubicle that contained two small sofas that could be made into a bed at night. We had a very nice reunion and were grateful that they had allowed him to come back through Tennessee.

When he reported to the base the next day, it was to find out that his squadron had been shipped out while he was gone so he was sort of hanging loose until they could decide where to send him. Within a day or two, we were on another train going to Miami where he would be assigned to a squadron that was being trained to invade Japan when the time came. So God had blessed us again with the promise of more time together. We found a nice flat on the second floor right on Biscayne Bay and I had a kitchen and could finally pretend that I was keeping house. We had travelled to Miami with another Marine pilot, Ken Grandchamp, from Connecticut, who had gotten separated from his squadron for some reason. So he was eating with us every night. But he was very unhappy and unsettled. He had met a girl in Jacksonville the night before he left there and felt he had fallen in love. So after listening to him groan and moan over having to leave her behind, I suggested that he call and tell her to come down and stay with me and Wil a week and maybe they could sort out their mutual attraction and the problems of being separated. She came and we became immediate friends, as I was alone all day in that big city. Her name was Barbara and she was living with two older sisters in Jacksonville as her parents were dead. She slept on a sofa in our living room. She was very sweet, was twenty-one years old, but acted like a teenager, and I felt like an old woman by the side of her. Wil called her "bird brain" in a joking way. Ken and Barbara were very much enamored with each other and after about three days, decided they wanted to be married so she could travel with him if possible.

Wil had bought a Chevrolet convertible when we arrived in Miami so we had everything we needed to enjoy the time in Miami. It was decided that we would go downtown to the courthouse and get their license and get them married. Ken called his family and got a lot of negative reactions from them. Ken was only twenty, he was Catholic, and Barbara was Baptist, and they had not known each other long enough. But Ken went ahead with his plans and had hung up the night before on his Dad, who was very upset with him.

Regardless of the reasons they should wait, they did not want to, so we were at the Courthouse that very afternoon. We ran into difficulties there also. Barbara was of age, but she did not have her birth certificate to prove it and she looked and acted so much younger. She had been spoiled and pampered by the older sisters, and they were also objecting to her getting married so hurriedly. They were told that the only place they could be married in Florida without the required proof of age was Everglades City but that was way down past the Everglades and the officials thought we might not want to try to go there. But we knew it all so we rushed back to the flat to pack overnight bags. Ken had been staying at the Room and Board House across the street but he had little packing to do and was ready and waiting for me and Barbara to be ready.

We were all excited, Wil and I could have cared less if they married or not but were willing to do our part to help them. It was a weekend and the boys were free and none of us had ever been to Everglades City. So it sounded like a very nice arrangement.

But the best laid plans often go astray and little did we know what was going to happen before we made our escape.

46 EVERGLADES CITY

We were almost ready to close our cases to depart for the unknown marriage haven when the doorbell to the flat rang out loudly. There was a speaker in the living room where you could talk to the person wanting entrance. So I called out, "Who is it?"

Some man asked loudly, "Is Ken Grandchamp there?"

Ken gasped, "Dad!"

I had no choice but to push the button from upstairs that would open the downstairs door and let Mr. Grandchamp in. We hurriedly pushed the suitcases under the bed in the bedroom and were standing around like four innocent children when he was welcomed into the living room. The poor man had traveled all night on a crowded train to get there to try to talk some sense into his son.

He lost no time in beginning his campaign and we all listened politely to him as he pointed out all the reasons why a wedding was a foolish thing at this time. He took us out to eat that night and he slept at the boarding house with Ken and took us out to a late breakfast on Friday morning. He talked and cajoled and begged and finally felt that he had succeeded in his mission and we took him to the train station about mid afternoon and put him on a train back to Connecticut. Then we hurried back to the apartment and finished packing to go to Everglades City. I had never felt so irresponsible in my life.

The sun was pretty low in the sky when we set out on our journey. We knew we would be about midnight reaching our destination but we felt we would have no trouble finding a place to spend the rest of the night or probably just head back to Miami and spend all day Saturday resting up from the trip. None of us had ever been that far south in Florida so we really had no idea where or what we were going to. Just four crazy kids in love!

By the time the sun had set and it was really dark, from the back seat where Barbara and I sat, I could see the road was pretty narrow and it looked as if water was very close to the shoulders of the road. It was muggy hot but we had the top up and were euphoric over how easily we had managed to fool Ken's Dad. Wil and I really thought Ken and Barbara were being foolish to marry in such haste, but we remembered how it felt to want to be together and couldn't, and we wanted everyone to be as happy as we were.

We were getting pretty tired by the time we finally saw the small sign on the side of the road announcing that we were approaching Everglades City. There were two or three stores, an ice house, one general store with a gas pump, a small church, and what looked to be only eight or ten homes. The town was poorly lighted with gas lamps but finally we spotted one house with a sign in front that read JUSTICE OF THE PEACE. So we pulled up to the sign at one o'clock in the morning. Ken got out and rang the doorbell. An upstairs window flew open and a very irate voice bellowed, "What do you want this time of morning?"

Ken told him politely that he and his girlfriend wanted to get married. The voice bellowed again, "I don't marry anyone at this time of night. Come back in the morning after 10 o'clock!" He slammed the window down. Ken rang the bell again and meekly asked, "Is there a hotel in this town?" "Keep headed south and you will see a sign about a block away." And the window slammed down again.

Well, we found the hotel, such as it was. The owners occupied the lower floor and rental rooms were up a flight of stairs. A woman answered the door in her housecoat and gown, with her hair up in pin curls. But she was nice and seemed happy to have someone who was willing to pay for the two rooms we needed for the rest of the night. Wil was very unhappy over having to sleep with Ken for the rest of the night and Barbara and I giggled and acted silly for about an hour and finally fell asleep. We were wide awake the next morning and had to go down the long hallway to a common bathroom, which was barely sufficient for just four visitors. I wondered what they did when all the four rooms were occupied.

We dressed and were fed a good breakfast by the people who operated the hotel. We went back to the home, where the Justice of Peace performed the license signing and the ceremony in less than twenty minutes, pocketed the $25.00 he received from Ken, and wandered off muttering something about "Crazy kids coming way down here in the dark through the swamp." I wondered what he was talking about. Wil and Ken did not know, and Barbara said she was from Georgia originally and she knew nothing much about South Florida.

We soon found out! Imagine our horror when we reached the Everglades. There was not enough room to meet or pass another car, only swamp water, and as far as we could see there was nothing but dead cypress trees reaching grotesquely toward the sky with Spanish moss hanging from the branches and snakes 6 or 8 feet long hanging from the same branches or coiled up on ragged stumps. Alligators were sprawled alongside the road, half in the water and half on the shoulder. Huge turtles swam around submerged so that their shells looked like stepping stones in the water.

We lost our euphoria in a hurry when we surveyed the road we had so blithely traversed the night before and the dangerous things that we had been surrounded with. If we had had a flat tire or exited our car for any reason I felt that we would have been swallowed up immediately and no one would ever know what happened. We had completed our mission and Ken and Barbara made the trip to Jacksonville with us three weeks later, when the boys were transferred to California with a three weeks furlough to visit their parents and make the trip West. It was decided that we would leave the Grandchamps in Jacksonville and they would visit a few days and then go to Connecticut for Barbara to meet her new in-laws. Then we would meet in Memphis for the trip to the new base in San Diego where the fellows would soon be shipped overseas. But with the little convertible we felt we would have a wonderful trip going out and then Barbara and I could get ourselves home someway after our husbands left us.

Again, just four crazy kids in love!! And God looks after young children and fools.

47 HEADING WEST

We left Barbara and Ken and traveled happily on to Nashville to begin about ten days with his folks and mine. I had the gas stamps that Wil had been able to procure to get us to California safely in my purse and we had money enough to make the trip if we were careful with it. Everything went fine after a couple of days with the Cordells in Nashville and then to Pulaski for our stay with my family. On the way from Jacksonville we had stopped to pick up a soldier who was hitchhiking home for his furlough. You never passed up a service man. He seemed very nice and he sat in the front seat with us as we traveled as I always sat as close to Wil as possible. In Chattanooga, we stopped to get gas and I used our stamp book to be able to get what we needed. I put it back in the outside pocket of my purse and felt it was safe. But when we needed gas in Pulaski, I could not find the stamps anywhere and I was so upset as I would not be able to go to California without them. We decided that the soldier had pocketed them as he exited the car right outside of Chattanooga and I guess he could sell them or use them to have a grand time while at home. Daddy managed to spare us enough gas and stamps to get us to Nashville and Wil went to the Rationing Board there and they had mercy on us and issued the necessary books for us to continue to head west.

While were visiting in Pulaski a place had appeared on my right foot, a dark looking lump and it seemed to be growing. So Wil insisted that I have it removed while at home before the trip,. I went to Dr. Booth, who had seen me through so many things through the years and he removed it. The next day the foot was swollen and I had an infection. Dr. Booth said there was no way I could make the trip with that happening. But I told him I was going if I had to crawl. So he did what he could but when we got to Memphis, I could hardly walk. Wil had to carry me around everywhere we went. But he was strong enough for the task and I was sure I would be fine going so far, just as long as Wil was there to look after me.

The newlyweds arrived in Memphis on the l6th and we were on our way to whatever lay ahead. Things went fine except for my foot and Barbara had developed a bladder infection and was very uncomfortable and whiny. Ken was not as patient with her as Wil was with me and I felt sorry for her.

The journey was uneventful except for the excitement of seeing all the beautiful parts of America none of us had ever seen. When we stopped for gas late the second afternoon, just as we were ready to enter New Mexico, Wil felt we were making excellent time. We had no trouble with the car at all and the weather had been very nice all the way. But the service station owner told us if we wanted to get across the mountains, we had to do it that night as a blizzard was coming in and it would be impossible to travel the highway after that ended. That was scary as the fellows had to be in San Diego by Christmas Eve or else be court-martialed. It seemed they were threatened by that anytime they breathed too hard, but Wil packed me and Barbara on the little backseat, wrapped a blanket around us, and he and Ken took over while I prayed and Barbara cried. She felt so bad and her reception in Connecticut had not made her feel welcome in the family. However it seemed that she and Ken suited each other so she was happy she was with us.

You have never been in a blizzard until you drive through one over the western mountains. The snow came so quickly and it did not stop as long as we were moving. And Wil kept us moving through it. We passed cars stalled with the snow piling up around them and some people were waving and wanting us to stop as they were stuck on the mountain until morning. But we did not dare to stop, as the little car was light enough to keep on top of the snow that was packing tightly as it fell, but we would never have been able to get any traction to start again, so Wil never let up on the gas. I often wondered what happened to all those people that night as the mountains were so high, the highway ran right along the edge of the ridges, and if you went over, you would have never known when you hit the bottom.

It was about 2 a.m. in the morning when we finally arrived in Albuquerque, New Mexico. We found a hotel which was just a step above the one in Everglades City. Wil had to carry me up a long flight of steps but we were all so happy to be safe and back on lower ground away from the danger of the snow. Wil had an Aunt Bertha, his Dad's sister, who lived in Albuquerque, so he called her before we got ready to begin our journey. She was so excited and insisted that we come by and she would have breakfast waiting for us so we decided to do that. Wil had not seen her in years and she was the only family he knew about on the Cordell side. She had married a Mr. Spence, but I do not know why they had decided to live their lives so far from family, and yet she had no one except for Dad Cordell. We had a wonderful meal, hot biscuits and country ham, scrambled eggs, a good old Tennessee breakfast and a short but good visit. Then we were on our way again.

My foot was really swelling and I could not wear a shoe. We were worried about it, but decided to wait until we got to our destination before seeing a doctor. We made it to San Diego with a day to spare before Christmas Eve. Jimmy and my cousin, Malcolm Jones, were both in San Diego with orders to be shipped overseas. Jimmy was going to the Pacific and Malcolm was headed for the European battles. But we were able to get together and have a day or two to visit from a little motel room we found there. Then the boys got orders to go to Santa Barbara. I did get to see a doctor in San Diego and he gave me some penicillin for the foot and dressed it well so it was a little more comfortable and I could put my weight on it by the time we got to Santa Barbara. That was just before New Year's Day 1944. We felt like we had been around the world.

48 CALIFORNIA BABY 1944

Word in Santa Barbara was that the Squadron they were in would continue to be trained for the invasion of Japan, whenever it came, so we felt we would be close to the ocean for a while anyway. We settled in by renting a rich couple's summer cabin in the mountains and I was keeping house again. Barbara and Ken had a small apartment in Santa Barbara and the base was in the vicinity of that city. We loved the mountain cabin, but except for one or two houses that I could see but not walk to, there were no other people up there. And I was afraid to go out when alone because of the wild animals that I knew had to be up there.

As soon as my foot got better, I had other problems. I was so nauseated in the mornings I could not stay up and Wil had to go to the base. So I started going down and spending the day with Barbara while the boys were at the base. That was fine except I was not good company. I was so sick most of the time. I finally went to a doctor, not one on the base, as Wil would not allow me to do that, but one that was all right for what ailed me. I was pregnant. I was so happy over that and could hardly wait for the nausea to pass so I could enjoy what was happening. But it seemed I just got sicker and sicker. Finally, Wil gave up the cabin and moved me to town which was some better. But about the time we settled in on that, another move was made. The

Squadron was being sent to a base close to the desert so they would practice under those conditions. The day before the move, Wil drove to Los Angeles to see about getting a place for us to live as I was really not up to the trip. I was so sick that day that I crawled to the bathroom and I was so dumb about my condition that I really felt that I had lost my baby. Wil was late getting back and I was scared to death something had happened to him.   I was so upset by the time he got home, and he was so tired and discouraged, that I felt I had to do better to make things easier on him. So I made myself get up and dress the next morning, packed what few clothes I had, and we made the trip to Los Angeles, leaving Ken and Barbara to follow with another couple who were being transferred.

And so another episode of our daily soap opera began, in the end of January 1944. California weather was wonderful and we could have been enjoying everything if I could just get straightened out. We spent the first night in Anaheim, California, in a hotel, wondering what to do next. My husband always seemed to know what to do, thank goodness. He left me in the hotel room the next day and he went to the Navy Mother's Association. They told him of a little single lady, up in age, who had fixed up a nice little apartment over her small home with an outside stairway and they felt sure she would rent it to us. Bless her heart, she did, but with misgivings when she found out I was pregnant and not doing well. She knew nothing about such things and could only tell me about a doctor in walking distance. He was a German doctor and she did not know anything about him. The following day, Friday, I took myself around the block to his office. His name was Dr. Kirstin. He told me I was going to lose my baby and he needed to put me in the hospital and do a D&C. That was all Greek to me, but I did not want to lose my baby, so I refused. When Wil came back, he felt that I should have done what the doctor wanted me to, as I had been pretty sick and still was. But God was still watching.

Jimmy came up on Saturday as he was still in San Diego and he was much smarter about everything than I was so he called Mama. Mama, Daddy, Nancye and Wil's sister, Evelyn, were on their way to California on Sunday. Meanwhile, Dr. Kirstin told me he would give me until the following Tuesday and then he would have to do something or he could not be responsible. So by Tuesday, I let him put me in the local hospital. But he ran into complications there. It was a Catholic hospital and the nuns would not let him do anything like what he was planning. He got angry, told me to get another doctor, and he walked out. The minute he dismissed me, the nuns began to give me hormone shots, and by the time my parents arrived on Wednesday, I was some better and maybe going to be able to keep the baby. The family went to church in Fullerton, California and met so many good Christian people who wanted to help. Another doctor was found, who could and would go along with the belief that I could get better, and sure enough, I did. But my folks were trapped for almost a month before they could safely leave us out there.

At the Church of Christ where they went, there was a registered nurse who was willing to take on seeing after me, and there was a woman, whose husband was a conscientious objector, but he was serving in a civilian capacity to aid the War, so she was alone in a two bedroom house. She worked nights so we were able to work it out that we would rent her extra bedroom, share the house, and she would be with me in the day time when Wil was away. So we made it from March to August in good shape. We were not moved anymore and nothing was said about Wil having to go overseas. He did have extensive training over the desert and we knew that it was only a matter of time. But the year in California gave us an experience we treasured for the rest of our lives together. We had our son out there and named him after Gerald Green and Truman Dykes, Wil's buddies who had been killed.

My parents and Nancye came again for two weeks when Gerald Dykes was born. He had to be a Caesarean baby, which was unusual at that time, but he was perfect. He weighed 8 lbs. 9 ounces, and was 20 inches long. He was more like his Dad than his Mom and I had another Cordell male to adore and love more than I loved myself. We were still living with the lady in Fullerton, Katherine Ping; and Mrs. Ellis, the nurse, was still such a good friend and so helpful.

Then Katherine's husband came home from wherever he was serving and they moved to San Francisco. So we were displaced with nowhere to go again, but during all this time out there, we had the good fortune to find Daddy's first cousin and his family. His name was Dolph Underwood and his wife was Edith. She was from England and was so happy to have some of Dolph's family nearby so she took over caring about us. She had a friend who needed someone to live in their house while they went east for a six weeks visit with family. It was a lovely brick house, but it was built right in the middle of an orange grove, and not a neighbor close enough to even walk to. We were happy to be able to live there, but I would have to be alone every day as Wil had to be on the base from dawn to dusk. I had Dykes for company, we thought it would be fine, and there was nothing else for us to do.

We got moved in, settled, and had one night there, but Wil went to the base the next day and he did not come home that night. I will never forget that night as it was so lonesome and I was surrounded by orange trees and I didn't know what else. Dykes had an inner clock that told him he needed a bottle of milk at 2 am every night. I received a letter the next day from one of Wil's buddies, or someone he had asked to write me, telling me that Wil had been sent to the desert for a week of intense training. We had been expecting that, but felt it would be later in the year. They never told the men ahead of time as they were not supposed to have anyone they were responsible for following them around. It was really hard, but I knew I had to do the best I could. The house was so new there was no phone service there and Dykes was giving out of milk and I was out of groceries. So I gathered my sweet little boy up and started walking toward where I thought the nearest house was located. I finally found it and they let me use their phone and I called Edith. Then the family there drove me back to my house and Edith arrived later with enough supplies for the rest of the week. So Dykes and I went through our first time together. He was worth everything I had had to go through to have him. I could not lift him to do much good, but he seemed to understand and he was such a good baby. His bed was a large clothes basket and we could put it on the back of the Pontiac coupe we had traded the convertible for and he slept just fine in it.

We stayed in the orange grove until the owners returned from their trip and then we were hunting another place to sleep. We found that with a couple who had one little boy and were expecting another baby. They had bought a new house and one bedroom was not furnished. We purchased a bedroom suite and a baby bed and lived with those people for about six weeks.

Then the week before Christmas, Wil came home with his orders to be shipped to the Pacific on January 1, 1945. They had five days, had to report back to the base by January 1, and were not allowed to go farther than 500 miles from the base. What were we going to do? I could not drive the car, and even if I could, I could not travel across country alone. There was no way I could ride a train so far with Dykes and a bus trip that far was out of the question.

We could hardly stand to think about being separated again, and the War had been so furiously cruel, with so many young men gone forever. We had been far luckier than we had ever dreamed of being when we married, but Wil was so quiet that I knew he could not bear to leave me and Dykes so far from home with no way to get back there. We sold our bedroom suite and baby bed to the couple, packed the car, and drove up to San Francisco to see the Pings, hoping they would have a solution, but no one did. There was nothing to be done.

Christmas Day was on Wednesday and we stayed that night and the next with the Pings. We had a tearful parting on Friday and left early in the afternoon. We were heading back down to Los Angeles with not a clue as to what we would do. We did not do much talking.

I knew Wil was working things out in his mind and I trusted that he would come up with some solution. I, myself, had gone to the Rationing Board and gotten enough gas stamps to get us to Tennessee. But Wil was not too happy over that as he was not supposed to go more than 500 miles from the base and he had to be back by New Year's Day. So for once in my life, I could think of nothing to say and was fighting hard to be brave.

When we came to the main highway that led west to Los Angeles and east to Tennessee, he turned the little red Pontiac east and I knew he was taking me home. I did not put up a fuss as I knew he had made up his mind and we would just have to take our chances on him getting back in time. I was praying with every breath. And God was listening!

49 MAD DASH HOME

We began our journey just before it began to get dark and we drove almost constantly, stopping for gas and bathroom only. When we stopped I picked up anything that was packaged for us to eat and we would eat as we watched the miles fly by. The speed limit at that time was 55 miles per hour but I do not think we ever went under 70 miles on the whole trip. Dykes would not drink cold milk so I would buy fresh milk when we stopped, pour some in his bottle. Wil would stop long enough to put the bottle in the space where the radiator cap was and drive five miles and the milk would be warm enough to satisfy our little one.

I was silent most of the journey and Wil had his mind on nothing but covering the miles. I could catch cat naps and tend to Dykes but was not much help with anything else. Wil had tried to teach me to drive but I was not good at it at all and had no license. But he got so sleepy at one time that he wanted me to see if I could drive for a while and let him catch a nap. When he awoke an hour later I was creeping along at about 30 miles per hour so that ended my driving as we could not take that much time. Finally, we gave a ride to a hitchhiking sailor and he drove pretty much of Saturday night. We were about over the mountain country at that time and there was more traffic. But the sailor drove even faster than Wil. He was enjoying having the little Pontiac at his command but I was keeping a close watch on him from the

221

back seat.

Somewhere along the way the next morning, we let our hitchhiker out in northern Texas and we continued our journey. It was Sunday morning and we were looking pretty scrungy and tired but we had to press on. When we got to Memphis, Tennessee we felt like shouting. We headed up Highway 70 to Nashville. I had called my folks along the way and informed them what we were doing and they were to be in Nashville on Sunday to meet us at the Cordells.

It was so cold when we got closer to Nashville and had about five inches of snow on the ground. But at least the roads were clear and we made it to Nashville and home late that Sunday afternoon. We had driven almost 2500 miles in 53 hours. Some of the family was at church and came in shortly after we arrived and it was a happy reunion and a sad one as we were all aware that Wil was soon to be fighting in the Pacific. I did not have a coat with me as I did not need one in California but Mama had remembered to bring me the red coat I had left with them. There was so much family there that night that it was bedlam but finally we all settled down to make the best of the situation. Our little coupe had no antifreeze in it as none was needed in California and it froze about the first two hours we were there but we had Daddy's car so we decided to not worry about our car until later.

We all stayed at the Cordell house Monday and most of Tuesday, the 31st. Wil had managed to obtain space on a plane to California that would leave at 9 PM that night. It was still so bitter cold that Daddy drove to Pulaski to bring Mama and the girls and Dykes home so that they would not have be out that night. Then he drove back to Nashville to be there with me when Wil left. It was so cold the Cordells all decided to say their goodbyes at the house rather than the airport. I felt so sorry for Mother Cordell as John Alton was already in the European war front and Clifford was over there also somewhere. Now Wil was having to go. Jimmy was already in the Pacific and had been for several months. So it was sad times for everyone.

Daddy took Wil and me to the airport and we were going

to head for Pulaski from there as soon as Wil was in the air. The airport was so crowded, mostly with boys leaving and their families hanging on just as long as possible. We were allowed to go to the plane with those who were departing back then. So I braved the cold wind and went with my dear husband to the foot of the plane steps. He kissed me goodbye and held me tight but neither of us could say a word. He turned and walked up the steps of the plane without looking back and I know he was crying just as I was. I headed back to the building and the tears froze on my face. Daddy was waiting with open arms and I fell into them crying, "Oh Daddy, I know I will never see him again. " Everyone in the airport was crying for me or with me. Such sad times.

Wil made it back to Los Angeles with a few hours to spare. Daddy and I drove back to Pulaski that night and so began the year of 1945 with me back where I started and Wil on his way to points unknown. He did have a week or two in California before being sent out and he managed to send me a beautiful portrait of him in his uniform as I had been after him to do that but he had kept putting it off.

Dykes loved being in Pulaski. He became king of his kingdom and his worshipers consisted of a Grandmother, Grandfather, three young aunts, and scores of friends and connected family. I was once again writing a chain letter to be able to mail it to Wil just as soon as he had an overseas address. I could hardly believe what he and I had done by taking the chance to drive to Tennessee, but I was so thankful and grateful to be with family if I had to be without Wil. And I was so thankful for the wonderful year, regardless of the hardships, we had had together. If nothing else, I would have memories of that year together SO LONG AS LOVE REMEMBERS.

50 BEGINNING OF 1945

The first week of 1945 was and still is a hazy time. I felt as if my life had ended with Wil so far away and Dykes and I back where I had always been but everything was different. We all settled in to wait for the boys to return and we had no idea when that would be or if they would ever return. So many who had gone over were gone forever, but hope springs eternal. So I settled with Dykes in my upstairs bedroom which was unchanged except for the addition of a nice baby bed.

Word spread quickly among those who knew the family and we had lots of company. Everyone wanted to see the baby and if I do say so it was worth their trip. Dykes set out to charm everyone he saw with his big smile and happy disposition. I was so proud of him and already he was showing signs of being a duplicate of his Dad.

After about a week or ten days, the Cordells came for the day and brought our little Pontiac to Pulaski. I was happy to have it sitting in the yard but did not have the courage to drive it as yet. I purchased a baby buggy so I could take Dykes to town with me when I wanted to walk around the Square. It was so big and heavy and we had to go down one hill and up another to get to the Square that I was worn out before I got there. I was much too small to push such a burden up a hill but I was too stubborn to admit it. So I made out with that arrangement for a few weeks.

One day, I decided it was foolish to have a nice car and not use it so I made myself drive it around a few days and then I went to get a license to drive. The Patrolman was very nice to me and he could tell I was scared to death. But I did not make any terrible mistakes and when I finally finished all the tasks he gave me, he said I had passed. After that I even got to where I would drive to Nashville to spend some time with Wil's family. I always had to take a sister along with me so they could watch out for Dykes for me as he was no longer content to stay in the clothes basket as he did on the Christmas drive home.

About two weeks into January, the dreaded call came from Wil that they were being shipped out and that I would not hear from him for an unknown time. I felt as if my heart would break but he was upbeat and assured me that he would be back. So I joined the other thousands of war widows who were biding their time and counting the days. My cousin, Corinne, was back in the vicinity as Uncle Gilbert and Aunt Louise had finally settled in Giles County so that she and her little daughter, Linda, could come and be with them until Corinne's husband, Shannon would return. Linda was only about two months younger than Dykes so they were company for each other.

I felt I needed to do something with my time besides help Mama around the house or take care of Dykes. He had so much attention from every direction that I seldom had any alone time with him anyway. So a call from an aging Optometrist, Dr Murray, asking me if I would be willing to take a job as his Office Girl and Assistant, was accepted. I was delighted. I hired a girl, named Sue, to help Mama with the house and Dykes, and I took the job. My hours were great, 9AM to 4:30 PM. I could give Dykes his breakfast and a bath before I left every morning and he always went back for a good nap after that. Then I walked home for lunch and fed him and played with him and then he had an afternoon nap until the girls got in from school and he was well entertained. Nancye was only five years old at the time so she was at home with him all the time and I do not think he ever missed me. Wil was not too happy for me to go to work but I was able to persuade him that I really wanted to and that Dr. Murray was in his seventies and such a nice man to work for. I was learning how to mount glasses to a frame and could even bore the tiny holes in them to mount the ear pieces. And anyway, we needed to save all the money we could if we wanted to have the chicken farm we envisioned having So he accepted my reasoning. I do not know what happened to the chicken farm idea, but it filled several pages of letters we wrote back and forth before we gave up that idea.

By February, Wil was stationed on Iwo Jima, that God forsaken piece of rock that so many boys gave their lives to take from Japan. As soon as the flag was raised on the island and a makeshift airstrip was constructed, the Marines went in. They had tents and were given daily supplies of K Rations and one quart of water to drink. Wil lost about twenty pounds right away.

Jimmy had been stationed on Tinian Island and Guam and he was part of the Marine Air Force that flew supplies in to the boys on Iwo. Wil was waiting for them to land one day as he knew that Jimmy might be on one of the supply planes. Jimmy walked right by him and did not recognize him as he had lost so much weight. Jimmy did not write anything about the stark existence Wil was under. But he would slip food in to him any time he thought he could get by with it. I was happy when I knew that they were seeing each other from time to time. And I shipped boxes of any kind of food I could get stamps for that would survive the journey across the ocean.

So the long wait began. The war struggled on but we were slowly defeating Germany and her allies. By April 15 of that year our armies had entered Germany and had discovered so many horrors that we had only heard mentioned in Newsreels and the papers. Over 6 million Jewish people had been gassed in the gas chambers in Germany as part of Hitler's plan to weed out any one not of German heritage and to further his plan of Germany ruling the world. By April 30th, Hitler and his mistress committed suicide in an underground bunker as he could not face the defeat of his ambitions and he knew that he would be hanged in plain view of the world if he was captured. Everyone hated him and the chaos and carnage he had caused in our world.

About that time, our family was thrown into a disaster of our own. We received word that Jimmy was in a hospital on one of the islands in the Pacific. He had been in a Jeep crash during a blackout and the driver of the Jeep had been killed. Jimmy suffered a severe throat injury and one ear was almost severed when he went through the windshield. We were all so upset as Jimmy was the apple of all of our eyes and Mama was so upset she could hardly function. We waited patiently to hear more but news travelled slowly and then we heard that he was being sent back to the States and would have a furlough at home to recover. So we anxiously awaited his arrival and great was our joy when we saw that he still had his big smile and good looks and was not as damaged as we had imagined.

Things were looking good for the war ending in Europe. There was no hope of defeating the Japanese any time soon but we were thankful for any blessings. Jimmy would have to return to the Pacific after his leave was up. We made up our minds to enjoy having him while we could.

Mary W. Cordell

51 WAR'S END

About the same time that Jimmy arrived home to recuperate, the family was shaken with another tragedy. Word was received that Staff Sergeant Robert Shannon was Missing in Action. That was Corinne's husband and we were all just devastated, but Corinne remained certain that he would be found and she patiently waited to receive word of that good news. Then she began receiving messages from his Army buddies expressing their sorrow over him being missing and many prayers were offered for his safe return. But that was not to be. It soon became apparent that their plane had been shot down. Shannon was a hero. He made sure that all the other men were safely out of the plane as it went down, helping them through the passageway. And then he seemed to disappear with the plane, and never surfaced again. We were heartbroken. He had never gotten to see his little daughter, Linda. Corinne never really recuperated from the sorrow of losing her husband.

The War was nearly over in Germany. On April 30th, Adolph Hitler and his mistress, Eva Braun went into an underground bunker somewhere in Germany and committed suicide. Hitler knew that the end had come for him and his evil reign. On May 7, 1944 Germany surrendered. And we turned our prayers and thoughts to overcoming the Japanese. We were told that it would take five years and one million of our men would die in trying to bring an end to

228

the conflict on that side of the world. I knew that Wil would be among the first to invade Japan and I was just sick with worry.

While Jimmy was at home, he decided to marry the girl he had come to love, Dot Long, a very beautiful girl, about five years younger than Jimmy but very much in love with my brother. They were married on June 1, 1945 at the Long's home in the country, and then we all came to Pulaski for the reception at our house on East Jefferson Street. The couple left at midnight to go to New Orleans for a day or two and then on to San Diego where Jimmy would embark to go back to the Pacific. Like most of us, Dot wanted to be with her new husband as long as possible so she went to California with him. And we settled down once again to wait and see what would happen next.

In Oak Ridge, Tennessee, there had been a very secretive operation in a small factory there. No one ever even wondered what it was used for and even those who worked there had no knowledge of what it was they were so busy with. But in late spring of 1945, as the War was ending in Europe, a large ship was loaded with two objects under much secrecy. The ship was named THE INDIANAPOLIS. The objects were loaded off the East Coast. The ship was unescorted as it began its slow progress southward. There were no escort boats, no fanfair, just slow movement around the southern tip of South America and then across the Pacific Ocean very much as if it were on a pleasure cruise. It had no radio contact with any other ships or any bases, so far as the public knew. In fact no one had ever heard of the ship.

An interesting thing happened when the ship was within 100 miles of Iwo Jima, but the story was not told until about sixty years later when Wil told his two grandchildren about it. I had known longer than that, because he had received a letter from the only other person who knew what had happened, Lt Dorman Chastain. Dorman was reliving that episode in a letter he wrote Wil several years after the War was over, but Wil never seemed to want to talk about it so I never tried to get him to. We all wanted to block out those years if we could.

Anyway, at 4 AM one morning in July, Wil was awakened and told that he was ordered to meet a ship that was approaching their island and he was to fly with the ship and watch for submarines or any other enemy boats or planes that might show interest in the ship. It was the Indianapolis. So Wil and his two Marines who flew with him as gunners and radio man were flying around that early in the morning, wondering why there were no escorts or protective vessels surrounding that large ship. Wil was sort of mischievous and he decided that the ship had to be carrying soldiers who would be used to fight the Japs, now that Germany was defeated. So he thought, "Yeah, they are all sleeping down there and I have to be up at this time of morning to see that they get to sleep. I think I will just wake them up". Now the Torpedo Bomber plane was a lumbersome thing and made a terrific noise when it went in to drop the bomb attached underneath. So Wil opened it up and made a swoop over the nose of the ship. A few officers were on deck and they shook their fists at him. He did not understand that as they usually were happy to see escort planes and would usually wave and cheer when one buzzed them. So he decided he would do it again just for aggravation so he made another swoop downward. That time they fired at him, with no intention of hitting him, but shook their fists again. So he went away and kept his watch from a distance from then on, not knowing what he had done to upset them. He dreaded to land when his time was up as he felt that he would be arrested as soon as he landed. But much to his surprise, no one said a thing so he kept quiet also. He did tell Lt. Chastain what had happened and they both decided it would be their secret. Wil did not know for a while just what was so important about the Indianapolis and why the secrecy.

The ship delivered its precious cargo to one of the islands which our boys occupied. Then they slowly cruised toward Guam Island, still without any radio contact. The Indianapolis was sunk before reaching its destination and without radio contact, no one knew about it. Twelve hundred men survived the sinking and they floated in the ocean for four days before it was discovered what had happened and where they were. Only three hundred men were rescued, the others being eaten by sharks or dying from the exposure to the heat and water and to whatever wounds they had suffered when their ship was hit. How fortunate for America that the precious cargo had been unloaded before the presence of the ship was discovered. The first Atom Bomb was loaded on the Enola Gay and on August 6th it was dropped on Hiroshima, Japan, killing an estimated l00,000 people. The second one was dropped three days later when the Japanese still refused to surrender even after seeing what we had to fight with. They had been told a few weeks before the first bomb was dropped that they could surrender or else be wiped off the face of the earth. But they objected to one word in the surrender papers they were asked to sign. Emperor Hirohito had refused to sign unless they deleted the word "unconditionally" from the surrender order. President Truman decided to let it stand. So the Japanese decided to wait. This was taken as a sign of contempt and Truman ordered the bomb to be dropped. But it took the second bomb to convince the Japanese that we could and would mop them off the face of the earth if necessary. They thought we had an arsenal of the deadly weapons but we had delivered the only two we had.

August 6th, 1945 is a day that anyone who is still alive in 2016 and lived through that day will remember and shiver inside while remembering.

Japan officially surrendered on September 2, 1945. The minute that word was received in America that the War was officially over, our town as well as all of the towns in America were filled with chimes, bells, horns, and shouts of jubilation; and cries of sadness over the ones who had lost their lives and their loved ones. I remember the day clearly. We were all in the front yard waiting for the signal that the papers were signed, and when the sirens began, I ran all the way to our church building to join in the prayers of Thanksgiving. Mama kept watch over Dykes for me. Corinne was at our house that day with Linda but she just got up quietly and

went home. I felt so sorry for her but my joy that Wil had
survived that awful conflict was uppermost in my mind as I
ran to the church. Now all I had to do was wait until he could
be sent home. That did not come very quickly. But at least
Jimmy had been spared having to go back into the fray. A
lot of prayers were answered.

From the Pacific

April 24, 1945

My Darling Wife:
Well, today was the sweetest girl in the world's birthday.
Perhaps I should have said old woman for that is practically
what you are. I knew I would someday be sorry I married a
woman so much older than I but I just had to learn.
Well, this has really been a wonderful day for me. I got
back down here (Marianna Islands) late yesterday afternoon.
And I don't think I could have been much happier if you had
been here waiting for me. It is almost indescribable how it
felt. When you live in Hell for so long and then move up just
one step from Hell, it makes that one step seem like Heaven.
I thought this was a pretty lousy place when I came here the
first time but I just did not know what a lousy place was.
I got here after supper time last night (I had trouble with
my plane) but they knew I was coming so they saved hot
chow for me. They had spaghetti and meat balls and I have
never tasted anything so good. They have lousy cooks here
but I ate so much I made myself sick so I hate to think what
will happen when I get back to your cooking or just to you.
I took 3 showers today. Just could not get enough of
that clean, fresh water. Sent all my clothes to the laundry so
now I'll have plenty of clean clothes, plus clean sheets to
sleep on. Try living in the dustiest place you can find without
taking a good bath for 7 weeks and sleep on the same
sheets all that time and you will see they get slightly soiled.

To really top things off, Honey, I had several letters waiting for me. Had about 5 from you and got another one today. Still haven't gotten your package. Most of the boys had packages waiting for them, but I didn't. I don't mind that too much as I will get plenty to eat here. As you can see I have already started getting stationery from you. I had scraped up enough to last till I got here but it is so heavy I can't write more than one page. So just keep sending this kind for I like it lots better. I can also get stamps while I am here so wait to send more.

I also got the letter with the pictures. Best pictures I have seen of you in a long time. In one of your letters you were patting yourself on the back about your long letters. So to keep you from breaking your arm, I'll help you out. They really are swell, darling, and I'll guarantee if you keep it up I will never fuss at you about short ones again. I will try to do better also down here.

You asked me in one of your letters if I remember little things about us. Darling, I bet I remember more than you do. Lots of times when we were together you would ask me if I remembered so and so and I'd say "No" just to make you tell me all about it. But most important to me are the little things I remember about you. Some of them are so trivial that they seem sillier than some of the things you remember about me. For instance, you used to call me "Horse" before we married. I never knew why. Then there are other things that you would do or say that you never meant as a favor or a compliment but they pleased me tremendously. I like to hear you call me Darling, which you seldom did but I couldn't say anything about it because I never called you Darling or Honey. I don't think I did before we married. If I did you can say you were the first because I know I never called another girl that.

One thing I don't like is your attitude toward our marriage. I mean you keep telling me how grateful you are that I wanted to marry you. If you want to be grateful or thankful then thank God that a person as selfish as I could love anyone more than themselves. I mean you make it sound like I did you a favor by marrying you. Mary, I will be *blunt but perfectly truthful. I don't and never have thought you were the most beautiful woman I have ever known. I do think you are pretty, have a beautiful body and are much prettier than any girl I ever dated. But regardless of what you looked like, I did not fall in love with you for looks. It was not for lust of the flesh either (except the first night I met you in Pulaski) because from the very start I thought you had the sweetest disposition and most pleasing personality I had ever seen. You were clean in mind and something I could be proud of. You were the first girl I had ever taken to see my folks. Even then I was deeply in love with you and you were to me something so perfect and different that I wanted to show you off and see just what Mom and the others thought of you. From the very first they all loved you. When I met your folks I could understand why you were the way you were. All of you were just alike. That made everything perfect for I wanted in-laws I could love like I did my own folks.*

The first time I kissed you, it wasn't like kissing any other girl. It was harder for me to kiss you because I was afraid you would object. But if you hadn't let me kiss you that night, I don't think I would have ever dated you again because you were so much better than I that it would have impressed me as your being too good for me. Anyway anything we did while going together did not mean anything morally wrong. I know everything you did was motivated by real love and not something cheap. I am very proud of both of us and the way we were with each other and glad that we never did anything that we had to hide.

So the greatest compliment you have paid me is to introduce me as your husband. I remember the first time I was introduced as Mr., Cadet and Lieutenant but none of them gave me the pleasure and satisfaction as when you first introduced me to someone on the street in Pulaski as your husband. That really saw a dream come true.

Well, darling, I guess I had better close for tonight. I love you so very much.

Your Wilburn.

Part of a letter Wil wrote July 8, 1945.

My Darling:

Well another Sunday and another day without mail. Unless you missed two days not writing I still have not gotten the letters for the 25th and the 27th but I have already gotten letters dated as late as the 30th.

Today has been just another day. I had the day off but I didn't go to church. I got up and went to breakfast. Then came back and went to bed again. I slept until about 2 o'clock, then got up and cleaned up my tent and my clothes. I started reading some of your old letters but didn't read them all. I think I had better save them, for you have been making some very rash promises in some of those letters. And what better way is there to hold you to them than to have it in writing? For instance, you have promised to serve my breakfast in bed (every morning), promised not to argue at all, and to let me buy a new car. They are just a few that come to mind but I have plenty more. Yes, when you hear and see all of your promises put into use at once, you may not be so happy to see me home after all.

Oh, yes, another thing you promised is that you would see that our family didn't get any bigger. I most certainly am going to hold you to that. (Doctors had said I should not have any more children. I was lucky to have little Dykes.)

I never had any intention of marrying Joyce but I was content with that arrangement. Then after I started going with you several things changed. First I liked a lot of things in you better than Joyce. Second, I already had Joyce and I still had to win you so that would have kept my interest if nothing else. Then I liked your family much better than hers. But most of all I liked you best of all.

I guess the night I carried you up to Granny's was one of the first nights that I was really sure. You were the first girl that I had cared a flip about whether any of my folks liked you or not. In fact, if they didn't, that just increased my interest more. If my folks didn't already know the girl they certainly never met her through me. But at Granny's that night I could see it in everyone's face that they liked you and I knew what everyone said to themselves, "Well, maybe the wild colt has at last decided to settle down with one nice girl." They did not want me to marry, of course, but anything was OK if I would only settle down. That was the only reason Mom ever agreed for me to marry and even she wasn't sure that marriage would change me much. And of course, your folks were even more certain that it wouldn't. If I had married Joyce, I know it would not have made me settle down because I did not love her and would not have been happy. And I have been so very much with you. I have given up a lot of things so I could be happy with you, but it has been worth it.

Mary, you will never know how much I really love you. But there is one thing that I am terribly afraid of. I have told you what it is several times so you should know what it is, and it has nothing to do with me being over here or the War whatever. It is mostly my fault, I suppose, but I don't know what to do about it. Maybe by the time I get back it will all be OK again. I surely hope so. (He was referring to the fact that he was very jealous of me and he never had reason to be and he knew it.)

Well, Darling, I got a letter from Jimmy yesterday and I want to answer it before going to bed so I'd better close . I love you with all of my heart.

Always
Wilburn

A Letter from Mary to Wilburn July 15, 1945

Sunday Night

My Darling:

I just finished giving the Skipper (Dykes) a glass of milk and thought he was going to sleep but he is up again walking all around his bed and is having a "confab" with his shadow on the wall now. He really is a card. One of the

236

little boys on the street gave a movie of cartoons today on a home movie set and the admission was ten cents. So the kids carried Gerald Dykes and his dime and he went to see the show. They said he really enjoyed it and I know he did as he gets such a kick out of the cartoons in a movie theatre. (I haven't carried him in a long time.) Paula said he just laughed and waved his arms.

I bought him some new shoes last night with real hard soles. Had to give a stamp for them. He has been used to soft shoes so I put the new ones on him last night and I guess they felt too heavy or "sumpin". Anyway, he'd crawl a few feet, then he'd sit down and start to cry, then he'd crawl a little farther and cry again so I finally took them off. But he's made out fine with them today. I think they will help him to walk.

I went to church both this morning and tonight. Aren't I getting good?

We had company all afternoon. Aunt Jim, Uncle Buster and Aunt Frances and two of her nieces, Corrine, Aunt Louise and Linda, two or three of the Pollocks and one of the nurses from the hospital were here all afternoon. I did get away to carry your letter to the train and to write to John Alton.

Corinne had a letter from another boy today and he told her they were still looking for Shannon. She just has so much hope that he is still alive that it is rather pathetic. I surely hope he is.

Darling, I've been thinking today of what you said about me and Joyce and the liberties I let you take. I didn't take exception to it or anything like that because I was convinced a long time ago that you understood about it. You do understand, don't you? I was never like that with anyone else and was only that way with you because I was so very much in love with you. But I like to talk to you sometimes about the things we did before we married simply because they were wrong, I guess and as you said it was because it was wrong that made it more fun. But Wil, I felt like, and I still do, that I was the one and only girl you ever did that way with. If I hadn't, I might have been less willing. The first time

*that you ever kissed me in such a way as to make me realize
I was in love with you was the night Thomas and Sarah got
married. That was the first time that it ever dawned on me
what being married to you could be like. From then on, I
could think of nothing but being your wife. And then that
night in November, when we almost got married and didn't,
we went a little farther, me letting you, in hopes that maybe I
could maybe satisfy what it was I wanted and quit thinking
about it. But that didn't help. It just made it worse. And that
longing tortured me till we were married and then our first
night together, I was afraid of you. I began to feel like I had
married someone I hardly knew and I didn't want you. I think
if you had tried very hard that night I could have gotten that
old feeling but we were both tired and you were not very
loving. I will be thankful to you the rest of my life that you did
not touch me that night. We might have gotten off to a start
that would have taken a long time to get over.*

*But the next day I began to feel the urge for that
something. I really never knew just what I had been waiting
for until that night that you came home after taking Chief's
body home. I can almost see you now in your red striped
pajamas and so handsome and clean and I loved you so
much. Still do, in fact. I loved you so much that I will never
be sorry for anything we did. In my heart and mind,
everything I did, I did with a clear conscience and it was as
innocent as the love I had for you. I know you know my love
was innocent because I was too dumb to be otherwise. I
didn't even know what it was I wanted where you were
concerned. I just knew that I wanted to belong to you. I
wanted to spend the rest of my life with you and be able to
ask you about things. I wanted to belong to you because
you were so handsome and because I was, and still am, so
proud of you. You were all I had ever wanted and you are all
I want now, So I am counting the days until you'll be here,
Darling, and I am not quite so innocent now as I know what I
want.*

*I Love You,
Your Mary.*

(Oh what an innocent time that was when loving was so personal between two naive and innocent souls. I really resent that movies, TV, magazines etc. have tarnished forever the kind of love Wil and I had when I thought hugging and kissing were so wrong. And I really was dumb in the ways of loving between husband and wife as it was never discussed at that time. I have always been happy that Wil could know that he was my one and only teacher. And he was a great one.)

52 REUNION

The month of August, 1945 was so tumultuous and exciting as we all began to plan to get back to living and having our boys home once again. But word from Wil was not so encouraging. He wrote that they were going to be held on Iwo Jima for a few more weeks as they needed the Torpedo Bombers to scour the ocean for Japanese submarines. So many Japanese were against surrendering that the government felt that they might try to load their submarines with enough soldiers until all of our troops were withdrawn and take the islands they had been fighting for. I was so upset as so many boys were coming home every day and getting their families together, and I wanted to be doing just that.

I gave up my job with Dr. Murray as soon as he could find a replacement. I spent my time filling my cedar chest (my hope chest) with things I would need for keeping house. I embroidered pillow cases, bought towels dish cloths, sheets and any utensils that I could afford. Jimmy and Dot came home from California and rented a house on East Jefferson, not far from where we lived. He went to work for Daddy at the station until they could decide what direction they wanted to go. But all I could do was keep on writing to Wil and hoping and wishing that he would be deployed.

By the first of December, I was really unhappy and so

was Wil. I was afraid that he would not get home for Christmas and I did so want him to be here for Dykes. And for myself. There was not much encouragement that that would happen. I couldn't stand to think of Wil having to spend Christmas so far from home and under such circumstances as they had endured all year on Iwo Jima. Iwent to bed on December 14th pretty discouraged.   Dykes was almost sixteen months old by that time and the only Daddy he knew was my father and another one who was a picture on the wall.

We were barely awake when the phone rang on December 15th and Mama called up the steps that I had a long distance phone call. I flew down the stairs wondering what had happened that I would be getting a phone call at that time of morning and scared to death that something had happened to Wil., Imagine my surprise when I answered and my big Marine husband said, "Mary, I just landed in San Francisco."

When I came back to earth, he wanted to know if could possibly come to California so we could have a few days to ourselves before being enveloped by family. I cannot remember all the plans and how they evolved but I was going to California if I had to walk.

Daddy had a cousin who lived close to Los Angeles and he and his wife and daughter had been really close to us when we were there in 1944 so Wil was going there and I was going to the Los Angeles airport and he would meet me. So by late afternoon, my and Dykes' clothes were packed and Daddy took us to Nashville. I found myself asking, "Am I crazy?" I had never been anywhere that far alone and now I had the responsibility of taking care of Dykes and flying over 2000 miles on my own.

Planes were not sleek and trim then as they are today. In fact, it was almost like being on a Greyhound bus with wings. It was so noisy when in the air, I could not sleep. We landed at every airport between Nashville and Los Angeles. Of course, there were not as many of them as there are now. But my baby was so good that when he was not sleeping, he was charming all the other fellow passengers. So he made the trip fine, all thirteen hours of it.

The airport was so large and so crowded. A Navy ship had just disembarked in the harbor and all the sailors were at the airport trying to get passage home. There was a sea of white uniforms and I felt lost in the crowd. The suitcase had no rollers as we do now so I had it, a makeup kit, my purse in one hand, and Dykes with the other. Every time I let him go, he would get away from me. Once he ran to a sailor and threw his arms around his leg, looked up into his face and said, "Daddy." He almost gave the sailor a heart attack, I am sure, but when I explained that I had talked of nothing else to him except that his Daddy was coming home, I guess he could claim any of them.

I finally gave up on meeting up with Wil and got a taxi to the cousin's home. Wil was still not back but there were no cell phones or any way to get word to him to come on back, We settled in to wait for him. Dykes and I were sitting on two footstools in the kitchen while Edith, the cousin's wife, was fixing lunch. We heard the car in the drive and the door slam. My heart was pounding with excitement.

Wil came through the door, his handsome face creased with worry, saying, "I couldn't find them anywhere." By that time I was running across the kitchen. He grabbed me and threw me to the ceiling and caught me when I came down. My arms locked around his neck and my legs around his middle. I thought my heart would just burst with happiness. The love of my life had made it safely back. It took a few minutes to make peace with Dykes as he thought the big man was hurting his little Mommy because she was crying. Edith and Dolph were as happy as we were. We stayed with them the rest of the afternoon and I put Dykes to bed and Wil and I went to a hotel to have our joyful reunion and make plans for getting back to Tennessee. By the time we rejoined our son the next morning, he had charmed all three of the cousins and did not even seem to have missed me.

It was decided that we would just buy a second hand car and drive ourselves home We thought we would take a week to make the trip and go over into Mexico for a day or two. Then we could sell the car when we reached home. That way we could have our precious time alone and then retrieve most of the trip expense when we sold the car. Famous last words – but we were too euphoric to care what the trip might bring. So Wil and and Dolph went to a man who called himself "Mad Man Muntz" and he had made a fortune fixing up used cars during the War and selling them to service men anxious to get to their families. Wil bought a 1937 four door Plymouth. It looked pretty good and seemed to be running fine. So we spent one more night with the cousins and began our journey to Tennessee early next morning.

53 THE JOURNEY HOME

We took a side trip to Fullerton, California to say hello and goodbye to good friends there who had been so wonderful to us in 1944. One couple especially who had helped us through my very trying pregnancy and birth of our baby. Their names were Clyde and Esther Ellis. She was a registered nurse and had two small daughters. They were our adopted family when in California as well as the cousins we had found.

After saying our goodbyes to everyone and to our sojourn in California we headed southward on what is now the I-10 Freeway and we were as happy as if we had good sense. The War was behind us, we had been survivors and even though Wil's squadron was held over on Iwo Jima we were finally together, a family again and that was all that mattered to us. Our life together was really just now beginning and we were full of plans and expectations as we began our journey home.

You have to climb a mountain at almost any point leaving California and we were heading up our first one when the Plymouth began to run hot. The first indication was a spewing of hot water that suddenly hit the windshield. Wil pulled over to the side of the road and raised the hood. The radiator was boiling. But my Marine always knew what to do so he waited until it cooled off before taking the radiator cap off. As we walked around the car and let Dykes play along the side of the deserted road, no one came by to stop and help us. About that time, we heard the air going out of one of the tires. Cars always had a pump in them in those days as tires had inner tubes and you could pump them up to get a few miles up the road. Wil pumped up the tire and we said a prayer that the other tires were not as near gone as that one was, as rubber had been rationed for so long that tires were still scarce and a premium. When the radiator cooled we made a reverse turn and coasted to the bottom of the mountain that we had just climbed. It was beginning to get late and we thought we were in the middle of nowhere.

But there was a house way over in a field at the bottom of the incline. It was decided that I would walk over there and see if I could use their phone and call Mad Man Muntz. A nice older lady named Mrs. Frye invited me in and was happy for me to use her phone when I told her our problem. Nothing was too much trouble if it would help one of our servicemen. But Mad Man Muntz did not have that mind set and he just laughed at me when I asked if he could send us some help. I proceeded to give him a piece of my mind about selling junk cars to the boys who had fought for his freedom while he stayed at home and sold those returning boys his junk cars so that they could make it home. And then he would not help them when the cars gave out within less than 500 miles of driving.. I was so upset and angry when I hung up that Mrs. Frye insisted that we just spend the night with them and her husband would help us get the car to a garage nearby the next morning. Have I mentioned how many Angels Unaware we had encountered during our marriage and our travels? Well, I should have as they were there all along the way.

So the first night of our "honeymoon" was spent in a sparsely settled part of California, with a very sweet couple who fed us a good supper, gave us a bedroom with a pallet for Dykes and a good breakfast the next morning. Mr. Frye took Wil to the garage and they were back before noon with the assurance that the car should take us on the journey we had planned. Mrs. Frye packed us a nice lunch and we set off again. Dykes was having a ball, unaware of the aggravation his parents were having, because we were so happy that nothing was really bothering us.

We were not even out of California before we were running hot again and that night found us in a small village garage. The owner spent the entire night trying to get the problem fixed. Dykes slept on an old car seat that was in the office. Wil felt sorry for me as there was nothing to do to fill the time and he was helping the mechanic. So he gave me six quarters and told me to play the slot machine.

I was certainly not ever a gambler but I shoved the quarters into the slots. On the third try, I hit the jackpot. I should have quit while I was ahead but you know how gamblers are born. I fed most of them back into the machines and was unlucky the rest of the night.

We were so tired by that time and had spent so much of the cash we had on the car, we decided that we had to forego the trip into Mexico and try to get ourselves home by the end of the week. So we stopped at a dinky motel (most of them were dinky back then) and slept for most of the day and started out again late that afternoon thinking it would be better to travel at night as the car might get too hot again. Even though it was December the weather where we were was pleasant and the nights somewhat cooler. That was a mistake because midnight found us sitting right on top of a mountain in the pitch dark with no other cars at all coming or going. We just sat there and talked and planned and waited for daylight to come so maybe someone would come along who could help us. It was almost morning when we heard a noise which neither of us could identify. It was a clank-clanking sound coming up the mountain and then a car pulled up behind us and four big Mexican men piled out and started to walk over. Wil got out of the car with the warning for me to lock the doors and not open them for anything. He walked back to meet the men.

I do not know how they communicated as they did not speak English and Wil did not speak Spanish but somehow it was agreed that we would put our spare tire on their rim (the cause of the clanking sound as they were running on the rim as they had no spare tire). Doing that, they would in turn push us into Tucson, Arizona, which was not too far away. So we arrived at a garage in Tucson about the time the city was waking up and we were in another garage for repairs. The man there looked at the car and said it would take a day or two to get it in shape to continue, but he had the cutest little Chrysler, with six tires, a small front seat, a smaller backseat, and a tiny trunk. A deal was struck, we paid the $125.00 difference, and said goodbye to Mad Man Muntz's lemon.

We had two days and one night on the road and things were going fine. We were still on Cloud Nine and as long as we were together, we did not mind that our honeymoon had been nothing but aggravations. The last day of our journey, we decided that we would just try to make it to Pulaski before stopping, so twilight found us somewhere in Arkansas, about an hour away from Memphis. Just as soon as it got dark and we had to use the headlights, we found that if we drove over 30 miles an hour the lights on the car would go off. So we had to stop in Memphis.

Wil pulled in at a filling station that was closed, where he parked the little car so that he could watch the highway, cut the motor and reached for me to get in as comfortable position as we could in the small space. Dykes was happily playing in the back seat and finally he went to sleep. He was such a good little boy. I did not question my husband's decision to sit right on the highway and tried to be patient.

Finally, a big semi-truck appeared on the horizon and I realized what Wil intended to do. When the truck went by, Wil was right behind it and stayed with it for the rest of the night. The truck driver kept signaling that we could pass him, but we couldn't as we would have been in the dark. Wil always knew what to do in an emergency, so except for making the truck driver crazy, it worked very well.

When daylight came, instead of being on Hwy 64 to Pulaski, we were on Hwy 70 to Nashville so we wound up having breakfast with Wil's family and a gathering that night of the Cordell clan rather than the Whitlock's. We finally made it home to Pulaski, parked the little Chrysler and did not try to sell it for several months. I hated to see it go at that time, but we needed the money worse than we needed two cars. It was a long time before we stopped talking about that trip and Mad Man Muntz.

We were finally home together for Christmas with the family and the whole world was before us. It would take several more books to tell all the adventures Wil and I had through the next sixty years, but even with all the sadness we had through those years, there were some very happy times and I will treasure all of them SO LONG AS LOVE REMEMBERS,,,,,

54 EPILOGUE: THE MAN I LOVED

How can I describe Wilburn E. Cordell (Wil to me)? It is easy enough to tell you about his good looks. He was 6 foot tall and weighed 160 pounds when I met him. He was all muscle without an ounce of extra fat on him. He carried himself like an ancient warrior and it was easy for me to imagine him dressed in the medieval armor that such men wore into battle. He had black wavy hair which he tried to comb back away from his face but there was one errant curl that would always fall down on his forehead and I adored it. His eyes were brown and had a sort of twinkle in them when he was amused or when he intended to play some kind of trick on me. Heavy eyebrows almost met above what I would call a patrician nose which suited his prominent squared-off chin. A large mouth that dominated the lower part of his handsome face revealed straight, white teeth when he smiled.

Wil was a hard working, hard driving sort of guy. His love of speed was a constant source of worry for me after I realized that he was the most important person in the world to me. He loved nothing better than to be behind the wheel of a car and he drove too fast. But he had a power of concentration that I envied and he kept his mind on the road. He never had a wreck except once when another car crossed the median and hit him head on, but that was in later years, when we had been married for almost 20 years. He wanted to fly a plane so badly, but lacked the funds for lessons, and certainly could not have afforded his own plane.

On December 8, 1941 he enlisted in the Naval Air Corps. He explained to me that if he had to fight, he wanted to do it from the air rather than the ground. He was afraid of nothing or anyone and I was afraid of everything, especially for him to be in the air. He tried to convince me that it was something he had to do. He would say that I was his first love, but flying came a close second. As usual I always came around to his thinking and gave in. He was not too happy when he realized that he could not get married until he received his Wings and commission and that would take about 18 months to accomplish. Our letters are full of the desire to be married and together and the back and forth of what we had to do for him to fly.

Wil was the most free-hearted man I have ever known. He would help people who needed it, regardless of how little money he might have. By the same token, he had no time for stupid people and those who took advantage of others. He dealt with the Teamsters Union for several trucking companies and the drivers would tell me that he was the fairest man they had ever dealt with. If the company was right, he would come down on the drivers but if the drivers were right, he was always on their side. That trait paid off for us when we started our own transport company in Florida and the drivers could have made things difficult for us but they did not.

When he passed away, our preacher said "Wil Cordell was a man of stature".

One of his Marine buddies used the exact words that I had used to describe Wil, when he wrote me a sympathy letter saying, "Wil Cordell was a gentle giant."

After he passed away, I was talking to our grandson, Davin, about Wil and I told him, "You know, when Wil walked in to a room where everyone was talking, people stopped talking until he was seated or had joined the crowd."

Davin replied, "It was because Pops had "presence", Tena."

I have to agree with Davin. Wil Cordell had presence.

ABOUT THE AUTHOR

Mary Cordell was born in Pulaski, Tennessee April 24, 1923, to parents Cecil and Ruth Whitlock, and a brother, James.

Because of the Big Depression, there were many moves made to find jobs – from Tennessee to Alabama to Cleveland, Ohio and then back to Giles County, Tennessee when she was ten years old. Three little sisters were added to the family by the time she was fourteen.

She was Valedictorian of both the 8th and 12th grade class in Pulaski and went to Nashville Business College on a scholarship in the Fall of 1941. It was there that she met Wilburn E. Cordell and both fell madly in love.

After December 7, 1941, she had to wait for him to serve his country and he enlisted to become a Marine Pilot. He received his Wings on August 27, 1943 and they were married August 28, 1943. She followed him from Florida to California for fifteen months, and their son was born in California August 31, 1944. Her husband was sent overseas January, 1945 and she and the baby came back to Pulaski to wait for him.

After the War, they lived in Tennessee, (Pulaski, Nashville, Knoxville and Kingsport) and in Atlanta, Georgia for ten years.

They ran their own transport company in Gainesville, Florida from 1967 until 1973, when they turned it over to their manager, and retired to Giles County after Wil's third heart attack. They sold the business in 1981 as their son was very ill at that time. They developed the Haywood Creek Subdivision in Giles County.

Their son, Dykes, passed away in 1996 from brain tumors. He was a Pediatric Cardiologist.

Mary's Wil, her husband for sixty one years, passed away on March 13, 2004 at the age eighty one.

Mary still lives in the house they purchased in 1977 on

East Jefferson Street, Pulaski, just four doors away from where they were married. Mary has several hobbies- reading, playing the organ, water coloring, collecting dolls, among others, but the main hobby of her life has been writing. She began writing poetry in the fourth grade, has kept diaries ever since that time, and she loves to write stories of all the wonderful things of life , including the sorrows, the sadness, the happiness, and the wonderful people she has known. She would not change any of it, except for the loss of her loved ones, but C'est La Vie.